The Louvre
French paintings

© 1982, 1987, 1989, 1991 Scala Publications Ltd.
Published by Editions Scala
14 bis rue Berbier du Mets 75013 Paris

Photography: Hubert Josse
Credit: Scala Istituto Fotografico Editoriale, Firenze

Distribution: SODIS

Colour separations: Scala
Printed in Italy by Graphicom, Vicenza
Dépôt légal janvier 1991

The illustration on p. VIII is reproduced by kind permission
of Documentation Française Photothèque.

Front Cover: Fragonard, *The Bold,* c., 1778.

Jean-Pierre Cuzin
Keeper, Department of Paintings

The Louvre
French paintings

EDITIONS SCALA

Contents

Chronology of principal dates in the history of the building of the Louvre and the creation of the Museum

1190 Under Philippe Auguste the keep and defensive walls of the Louvre are built on a site which is now the south-west corner of the Cour Carrée.

1214 The keep is used to house the royal treasure, archives and furniture store, and also as a prison.

1365–70 Under Charles v the château is extended to the north and east; the keep is now entirely surrounded by buildings. It is sometimes used as a royal residence but the court is based in the Hôtel Saint Paul to the east of Paris.

1527 François i makes the Louvre his official residence; the keep is destroyed.

1546 At the end of his reign François i commissions Pierre Lescot to rebuild the Louvre. The King's collection of paintings is to stay in the Château de Fontainebleau until the middle of the seventeenth century.

1547–49 Under Henri ii the Aile de Lescot is completed (south part of what is now the west wing of the Cour Carrée), decorated by the sculptor Jean Goujon; the Pavillon du Roi is built on the site of the Salle des Sept Cheminées.

1559–74 Continuation of work on what is now the south of the Cour Carrée.

1564–74 Catherine de Médicis commissions Philibert Delorme to build a château outside the walls of Paris, called the Tuileries.

1566 Construction of the Petite Galerie (now the Galerie d'Apollon).

1595–1610 Under Henri iv, the Grande Galerie is built, designed by Louis Metezeau and Jacques ii Androuet du Cerceau, and the new Château des Tuileries is linked to the Vieux Louvre.

1624–54 Under Louis xiii the Pavillon de l'Horloge is designed by Jacques Lemercier. It is attached to the Aile de Lescot, and to balance this wing another symmetrical one is built to the north.

1641–42 Nicolas Poussin is commissioned to decorate the vaulted ceiling of the Grande Galerie with scenes from the life of Hercules; after initial plans the project is abandoned.

1659–65 Louis Le Vau builds the north and south wings of the Cour Carrée.

1661–70 Le Vau builds the Galerie d'Apollon after the fire in the Galerie des Rois, on the first floor of the Petite Galerie.

1664–66 Le Vau and François d'Orbay make major changes and enlargements to the Château des Tuileries.

1667–70 The Colonnade, the eastern façade of the Louvre, is designed by Le Vau, d'Orbay and Claude Perrault. The façade by Le Vau to the south is concealed by a new one designed to be in keeping with the Colonnade.

1674 Works on the Louvre abandoned; from 1678 to 1789 the Château de Versailles is to be the residence of the King and Court. Organised almost like a museum, the royal collection of paintings is brought together in the Louvre and the Hôtel de Gramont attached to it. Gradually the pictures are distributed to the various royal residences.

1180–1223 Philippe Auguste

1364–80 Charles v

1515–47 François i

1547–59 Henri ii

1559–60 François ii
1560–74 Charles ix

1574–89 Henri iii
1589–1610 Henri iv

1610–43 Louis xiii

1643–1715 Louis xiv

1715–74 LOUIS XV

From 1725 The official exhibition of the Académie Royale de Peinture et Sculpture takes place in the Salon Carré of the Louvre, from which comes the name 'Salon'. These Salons took place until 1848.

1754 Jacques Ange Gabriel starts transformation of the second floor of the Cour Carrée.

1755 Public exhibition at the Palais du Luxembourg of a selection of paintings from the royal collection.

1755–74 Demolition of the old residence area around the Cour Carrée and Colonnade.

1774–92 LOUIS XVI

1774 The Comte d'Angiviller becomes Surintendant des Bâtiments du Roi; studies and projects for the creation of a 'Muséum' in the Grande Galerie.

1777 The 'plans and models' of royal châteaux which filled the Grande Galerie are cleared away.

1784 Hubert Robert, Conservateur des collections du Roi, is given responsibility for the organisation of the 'Muséum'. Top lighting installed in the Salon Carrée. The King once again lives in Paris: Louis XVI resides in the Château des Tuileries.

1789 FRENCH REVOLUTION

1791–92 After the French Revolution the royal collection becomes the national collection. Seizures of works of art from churches, convents and the nobility. A commmittee of artists continues the preparations for the opening of the 'Muséum'.

1793 The Museum Central des Arts is opened. A 'special museum for French painting' is instituted in the Château de Versailles.

1796–1807 An enormous influx of works of art into the Louvre, surrendered by or commandeered from Holland, Italy and Germany during the Napoleonic wars.

1800 Napoleon Bonaparte moves into the Château des Tuileries.

1804–1815 NAPOLEON I

1802–15 Vivant Denon Director of the museum which, in 1803, is renamed the Musée Napoléon.

1806 Construction of the Arc de Triomphe du Carrousel, the monumental gateway to the Château des Tuileries designed by Percier and Fontaine.

1810–14 Construction of the north wing of the Louvre along the rue de Rivoli, also designed by Percier and Fontaine.

1815–24 LOUIS XVIII

1815 After the battle of Waterloo all the works of art that had been surrendered by or commandeered from foreign countries are returned, except about a hundred paintings, mostly Italian, which stay in the Louvre.

1818 The Galerie royale du Luxembourg is created exclusively for the display of work by contemporary artists (subsequently the Musée du Luxembourg).

1824–30 CHARLES X

1827 The Musée Charles X is created in the southern wing of the Cour Carrée.

1830–48 LOUIS-PHILIPPE

1838 Inauguration of Louis-Philippe's Musée Espagnol in the eastern wing of the Cour Carrée.

1848–51 SECOND REPUBLIC

1848 The Second Republic decides to complete the Louvre as a 'palace of the people' devoted to the sciences and arts. Restoration and redecoration by

Duban; Eugène Delacroix commissioned to execute the ceiling painting for the vault of the Galerie d'Apollon.

1851 Inauguration of the new rooms.

1852 Baron Haussmann orders the demolition of the old residential area between the Château des Tuileries and the Louvre.

1852–70 NAPOLEON III

1852–57 Construction of the 'new Louvre' by Louis-Tulluis Visconti and later Hector Lefuel; the two palaces are linked together to the north by a series of buildings, thus closing the square with the Arc du Carrousel at the centre. New wings are constructed on either side of the Cour Napoléon producing large courtyards and allowing top lighting to be installed.

1861–70 Reconstruction by Lefuel of the Pavillon de Flore, decorated by Jean-Baptiste Carpeaux, and the western end of the Grande Galerie. The monumental triple arch through the southern wing is constructed.

1870–1940 THIRD REPUBLIC

1871 During the Commune (March–May) the administration of the museum is undertaken by a group of artists, including Gustave Courbet, Honoré Daumier and Félix Bracquemond. The Château des Tuileries is burnt out; the shell is not demolished until 1883 when the view from the Arc du Carrousel to the Arc de Triomphe is revealed.

1895 The Réunion des Musées Nationaux is created with autonomous financial powers respecting purchases. It is run by the Counseil des Musées Nationaux.

1897 Foundation of the Société des Amis du Louvre.

1914–18 FIRST WORLD WAR

1927 Under the authority of Henri Verne, Directeur des musées, a vast plan to reorganise the collection is begun. The decoration of the Grande Galerie is completed using Hubert Robert's designs.

1939–45 SECOND WORLD WAR
1945–58 FOURTH REPUBLIC

1945 The collection is brought back having been evacuated during the war and the exhibition rooms are gradually reopened.

1953 Installation of Georges Braque's triple composition *The birds* in the ceiling of the Salle Henri II replacing that by Merry-Joseph Blondel (1822).

1958 FIFTH REPUBLIC

1961 The galleries for nineteenth-century art are opened on the second floor of the Cour Carrée.

1969–71 The galleries in the Pavillon de Flore and the Aile de Flore are opened.

1971 The first of a series of documentary exhibitions, 'Files from the Département des Peintures'.

1972 A law is instigated allowing the presentation of works of art in lieu of death duties.

1984 Start of the 'Grand Louvre' project in the Cour Napoléon. This comprises a vast underground entrance hall lit by a glass pyramid, designed by the architect I. M. Pei.

1989 Inauguration on 30 March of the underground space below the Cour Napoléon, lit by the pyramid of I.M. Pei, and comprising entrance hall, rooms for temporary exhibitions and rooms devoted to the history of the Louvre; opening to the public of the adjoining crypt in the old moat of the medieval chateau.

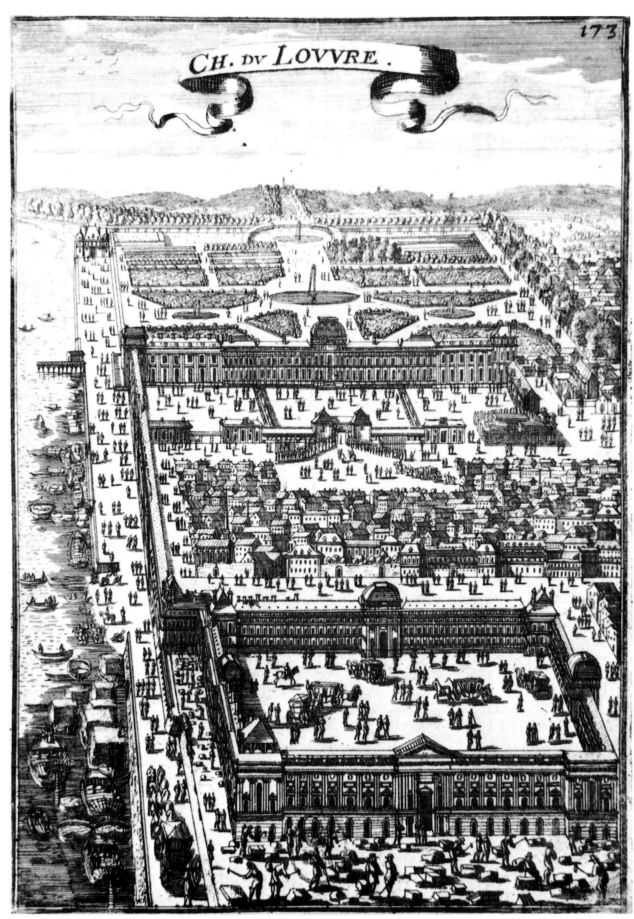

CH. DV LOVVRE.

Anonymous, *View of the palais du Louvre and Château des Tuileries in the seventeenth century*, late seventeenth/early eighteenth century

French paintings in the Louvre

GIUSEPPE CASTIGLIONE, *View of the Salon Carré in 1861*, 1861

The Salon Carré, at the eastern end of the Grande Galerie, is one of the most famous rooms in the Louvre. The official exhibitions of contemporary French paintings mounted by the Académie Royale de Peinture et de Sculpture were held here from their inception at the beginning of the eighteenth century until the mid-nineteenth century. It was this tradition that gave rise to the name 'Salon' for temporary exhibitions of paintings. Castiglione's painting shows the room just after 1851 when it had been redecorated and given a sumptuous new ceiling by Duban and Simart. The Salons now took place elsewhere and the dense display of paintings in this picture comprises a selection of the most renowned masterpieces in the Louvre at the time—all schools of painting and periods mixed together. Today the Salon Carré is devoted entirely to French fifteenth- and sixteenth-century art.

Introduction

The French paintings in the Louvre represent well over half the Museum's entire collection; their quality and fame make them by far the most important extant collection of such works. It was therefore decided to divide the Louvre's great paintings into two parts, and that the first of them should be devoted solely to the French School. It should, however, be emphasised that the Museum's other collections, such as the Italian, could well have merited this preeminence, since chronologically the scope of these two parts does not go much beyond the middle of the nineteenth century and, therefore, excludes the Impressionists and Post-Impressionists. The second part, *European Paintings in the Louvre*, covers the Museum's wealth of works from countries other than France and with the first provides for the reader a balanced view of the collection as a whole. In the following pages we shall trace the history of the Louvre itself and of its unique range of French paintings from the beginning of the sixteenth century to the end of the twentieth. Apart from Watteau in the Wallace Collection in London and in Berlin-Charlottenburg, and Bourdon in the Hermitage in Leningrad, there is scarcely any French artist that can be more fully studied elsewhere than in the Louvre.

We know that François I brought artists from Italy to decorate the Château de Fontainebleau and that he collected Italian paintings. He chose works by Leonardo da Vinci rather than contemporary ones by French artists, such as the Master of Moulins. Probably the only French paintings we would have found in the royal collection would have been family portraits. One still exists and is preserved in the Louvre—the portrait of François I himself, attributed to Jean Clouet (p. 18), which has now become the symbol of the continuity of the Louvre, a national collection which grew out of the royal collection.

It was not until the reign of Henri IV, after a long period of civil war, that another king was interested in art and commissioned paintings: some of those by Dubreuil which decorated the Château Neuf, Saint-Germain-en-Laye, have survived (p. 24), but we can really only talk about vestiges of a decorative scheme rather than a collection of paintings. Louis XIII commissioned works from Simon Vouet and asked Nicolas Poussin to decorate the Grande Galerie in the Louvre, as well as commissioning a large altar-piece from him (p. 38), although Louis XIII was not really a collector.

It was Louis XIV who enthusiastically resumed the traditional rôle of patron of the arts that had been established by François I. His reign saw the true beginnings of the Louvre's collection of French paintings, and it was dominated by four contemporary artists, two living in Rome, Poussin and Claude, and the King's two official painters, Le Brun and Mignard. After the death of Cardinal Mazarin in 1661, 546 of the former Prime Minister's most beautiful paintings became part of the King's collection. Of these 77 were French, although unfortunately their titles are not known. Throughout Louis XIV's reign many marvellous works by Poussin and Claude were bought or given to the king. Le Brun, Garde des tableaux du Roi until his death, prepared the first inventory of the royal collection in 1683 and another more systematic one was produced by the miniaturist Bailly in 1710. He catalogued 2,376 paintings of which 898 were copies, anonymous, of dubious attribution, or by Le Brun, Verdier and Mignard. Of the 1,478 paintings which constituted the main collection, the vast majority were French. Many, however, were not easel paintings but decorative works for the royal châteaux. The Cabinet du Roi (the King's art collection) was in the new part of the Louvre created by Le Vau, but these paintings were gradually dispersed to Versailles and other royal residences.

Louis xv, unlike his contemporaries the King of Prussia, the German princes, the Tsarina and the Queen of Sweden, was not a great lover of paintings; in 1770 the fabulous Crozat collection belonging to Baron de Thiers was sold in its entirety to Catherine the Great of Russia. Apart from a few paintings purchased from the Carignan estate, the royal collection was augmented only by canvases or tapestry cartoons commissioned to decorate the royal residences. Nevertheless, this means that the Louvre now owns important paintings by Boucher, Lancret, Vernet, Oudry, Van Loo and Fragonard.

On the other hand, it was during Louis xv's reign that it was decided to show part of the royal collection to artists and the public, a real innovation. From 1750–79, 110 paintings were exhibited in rooms in the Palais du Luxembourg, open at the same time as Rubens' Galerie Médicis, two half-days a week. Among the canvases displayed in this embryo museum, forerunner of the Louvre's, were a variety of French paintings—eleven by Poussin, four each by Claude and Valentin, and one or two each by Vouet, Le Sueur, Le Brun, Rigaud, Antoine and Noël Coypel, Mignard, La Fosse, Santerre, Vivien and Lemoyne.

Louis xvi's reign was decisive for the royal collection and would certainly have seen the opening of the Louvre museum had it not been for the French Revolution. In 1774, the year of the King's accession to the throne, the Comte d'Angiviller became Surintendant des Bâtiments du Roi, an appointment which included control of the royal collection. He realised the rôle that earlier masterpieces could play in 'reviving' French painting and to this end planned to open a 'Muséum' in the Grande Galerie of the Louvre. He tried to fill the gaps in the collection and systematically ordered works to be reframed in an attempt to unify the paintings. This constituted the birth in France of modern theories of museum conservation and display. French paintings were often purchased: not only history paintings commissioned from contemporaries, but also earlier seventeenth-century works, notably the cycle depicting the life of St. Bruno by Le Sueur.

The Muséum Central des Arts finally opened in the summer of 1793, during the Convention. Louis xvi's collection became that of the nation, and the revolutionary leaders, despite enormous immediate difficulties, were sufficiently enthusiastic to bring to fruition an enterprise that had begun under the monarchy. The concept of the museum, which had been growing throughout Europe, now came to fruition. At the Louvre, however, its realisation took on proportions which no-one could have dreamed of during the Ancien Régime. To the royal collection were added vast numbers of works seized from churches, convents and the nobility, as well as the works which had constituted the collection of the Académie Royale de Peinture et de Sculpture. A museum committee, consisting chiefly of artists, decided which works to keep for the Louvre. When the museum opened the paintings were hung in a very surprising mixture of periods and schools. Among the French paintings were several by Le Sueur and Vernet, examples by Poussin, Vouet, Patel, Champaigne, Valentin, Dughet, Bourdon, Mignard, Jouvenet and Desportes, two by Trémolières, a small Subleyras, a Vignon (now in Grenoble) and even a work by Tournier, then attributed to Manfredi (now in Le Mans). The earliest French painting was *The Last Judgement* by Jean Cousin the Younger, which had come from the convent of the Minimes, Vincennes.

So many works had now been gathered together that from 1793 a second museum had to be instigated at the Château de Versailles. This was the Musée Special de l'école Française, where in particular the election pieces of past and present Academicians were featured. The account of 1802 mentions 352 pictures: twenty-three by Poussin, ten by Le Brun and seven by Mignard, also examples by Vouet, Bourdon, the cycle by Le Sueur, Claude, La Fosse, Subleyras, Jouvenet, Rigaud, Chardin, Doyen, Tocqué, Van Loo, Lagrenée and Vernet. Among the contemporaries were Fragonard, Greuze and Vien. In 1804 this short-lived museum was disbanded.

However, the enormous assemblage of paintings in depots and in the Louvre was only the beginning. The victorious armies of the Republic and then the Empire commandeered the most prestigious works of art from royal collections and religious establishments throughout Europe, notably from Italy and, later, Germany. During the Empire Vivant Denon was the organiser and overseer of this unique museum. Thus, for a short time the Muséum, which had become the Musée Napoléon, owned a great part of Europe's heritage. It is interesting to note that at this stage the amount of space given to French paintings was small. In the Grande Galerie four bays were devoted to Northern Schools, four to Italian, but only one to the French.

After the Battle of Waterloo the Napoleonic dream evaporated and most of the booty in the museum was returned to its places of origin. Although the Louvre was singularly depleted, this dismantling was not fatal to the collection for, attached to the Civil List, the parliamentary allowance for sovereign's expenditure, it became once again the direct concern of the King. During the reign of Louis XVIII many of the works seized from the nobility and churches were retained by the Louvre, now seen as a great national institution. From this time on the collection turned more towards French painting; from the Palais du Luxembourg, at the same time as the Médicis series by Rubens, came the St. Bruno cycle by Le Sueur and several of Vernet's *Ports of France*. Some contemporary canvases were also purchased (David, Girodet, Guérin), and housed in the Musée du Luxembourg, which had been opened in 1818 for the works of living artists.

The most important project during the reign of Louis-Philippe was the formation of the Musée historique de Versailles, and the Louvre was somewhat abandoned. However, after the brief Republic of 1848, when it was again proposed, as it had been during the Revolution, to turn the Louvre into a 'palace of the people' including the museum, the Bibliothèque Nationale and temporary exhibition space, the Second Empire was to see one of the greatest epochs in the history of the museum. With the impetus of the Emperor behind the project, the vast Tuileries/Louvre ensemble was completed in record time, including the gigantic painting galleries (Salle Mollien, Salle Daru and Salle des États) which were such a novelty. Of the highly valuable acquisitions made during this period, the Denor La Caze collection in 1869 was the most important. Comprising some eight hundred paintings, it was the finest collection ever bequeathed to the Louvre. La Caze's contribution was inestimable in the field of French seventeenth- and eighteenth-century painting; one cannot imagine how, without him, the work of Largillière, Watteau, Chardin or Fragonard would have been represented today.

With the declaration of the Republic the Louvre became France's national museum and has remained so ever since; gone was the ambiguity of a museum funded by the Civil List of a sovereign. From that time on the purchase of paintings was gradual and methodical, acquisitions being made as knowledge of French painting was extended by art historical research. The generosity of collectors continued; gifts and bequests increased. It was, for example, collectors such as Thomy Thiéry (1902), Moreau-Nélaton (1906), Chauchard (1910) and Camondo (1911), whose gifts of whole rooms of paintings (often filling gaps left by official purchases) to a large extent formed the unrivalled collection of nineteenth-century art now owned by the Louvre. Also important are the collectors' contributions to early French painting such as those of: Schlichting (1914), Robert (1926), Croy (1930), Jamot (1941), Beistegui (1942), Gourgaud (1965), Lyon (1961) and Schlageter and Kaufmann (1984).

Above all, the magnificent support of the Société des Amis du Louvre, founded in 1897, has led to the acquisition of some of the greatest masterpieces of French painting, from the *Pietà d'Avignon* (1905) to La Tour's *St. Sebastian* (1979). The recent law allowing the donation of works of art in lieu of death duties has meant that major works by Champaigne, Fragonard, Greuze, Prud'hon and Courbet have been preserved for the nation.

With the opening, in the Spring of 1989 of the new rooms on the second floor of the Cour Carrée, the appearance of the rooms devoted to French art has almost completely changed. Our collections, from the fourteenth century to the end of the nineteenth century, are now much more amply displayed with many works brought out from the reserve collections, notably the large-scale seventeenth century works of Le Sueur, Philippe de Champaigne, Le Brun and Jouvenet, at last rescued from unworthy oblivion. In the near future, the rooms of the East and South wing, devoted to the eighteenth and nineteenth centuries, will be opened and the visitor will thus be able to walk around a complete circuit illustrating the history of French painting. The big nineteenth century paintings will remain in the admirable first floor rooms, Salle Daru, Salle Denon and Salle Mollien while, provisionally, the middle-sized French paintings of the eighteenth and nineteenth centuries are hung in part of the Grande Galerie and in the adjacent rooms of the Mollien wing.

When the changes are completed, the whole perception of French painting will be altered, due to the more complete exhibition of our treasures, and notably to the presentation of the great showpieces. The concept of French painting depends largely on what is seen in the Louvre, a concept which we at the Museum should constantly be broadening, redefining and varying, by drawing on the collection, enriching it still further and making it accessible to everyone.

The primitives and the sixteenth century

The great exhibition of 1904, devoted entirely to French primitive painting, established the importance and originality of those artists working before the sixteenth century. The study of fourteenth- and fifteenth-century Italian, Flemish and German painters had come well before that of their French contemporaries, and French works were therefore often attributed to other schools. In fact the concept of 'French primitives' scarcely existed before the twentieth century. Works by Van Eyck and Fra Angelico were exhibited in the Musée Napoléon but not those by Fouquet or Quarton, and the formation of the Louvre collection reflects the fact that in the history of taste French medieval art is very much a new arrival.

However, we should note a few paintings of prime importance that came into the national collection during the reign of Louis-Philippe. These paintings for the Château de Versailles, where the King was forming the Musée historique dedicated to 'all the glories of France', were purchased as historical documents: portraits of *Charles VII* and *Guillaume Jouvenel des Ursins* by Fouquet (pp. 12 and 13) and of *Pierre de Bourbon* by Jean Hey. Only the sitters were considered interesting and, *Charles VII* was even bought as a 'Greek work', implying that it was Byzantine! These pictures were only later transferred to the Louvre as works of art in their own right.

In the second half of the nineteenth century, just as the history of these works was beginning to be written, succeeding keepers of the collection bought new works and collectors gave others which are still among the most important in the Louvre. *The Narbonne altar-frontal* (p. 9) was purchased in 1852, in 1863 Frédéric Reiset gave *The St. Denis altar-piece* by Bellechose (p. 11) and Malouel's *Pietà* (p. 10) was bought the next year.

But it was the year 1904 which saw the real awakening of interest in French medieval art. The Louvre acquired *The Boulbon altar-piece* (p. 17), *The Paris Parlement altar-piece* (p. 15) and Jean Hey's *A donor and St. Mary Magdalen* (p. 14). The next year the great masterpiece *The Villeneuve-les-Avignon Pietà* (p. 16) was presented by the Société des Amis du Louvre. After that only occasional acquisitions were made, and the portrait of *Jean le Bon* (p. 9) was offered on extended loan from the Bibliothèque Nationale in 1925. Two extremely rare little paintings, a *Virgin* by a Burgundian master and *Charles-Orlant* by Jean Hey (p. 14), were part of the collection given by Carlos de Beistegui in 1942.

It is important to emphasise the extreme rarity of French primitives owing to their destruction during the Revolution and above all because of the late appreciation of these works by historians. This rarity makes us especially grateful for recent acquisitions such as *The Crucifixion with a Carthusian monk* by Jean de Beaumetz (p. 10) and *The Presentation of the Virgin* by Nicolas Dipre (p. 17), works by artists not previously represented in the Louvre, and *The Crucifixion* by Josse Lieferinxe (p. 17), an artist previously represented only by secondary work. Only in the Louvre can such a comprehensive collection of these rare primitives be seen.

The collection of French sixteenth-century painting is also comparatively recent. The glorious exception is the portrait of *François I* attributed to Jean Clouet (p. 18) which has been part of the national collection ever since it was painted for its royal sitter in about 1530. The royal collection must have comprised many portraits: the inventory drawn up by Bailly in 1710 mentions '251 small portraits of the families of past kings and nobility'. All that is left in the Louvre is a small full-length depiction of Henri II, a studio copy of the painting in the Uffizi, Florence. Of great importance to the Louvre is the enormous collection of works of historical interest, mostly prints and drawings, bequeathed by Roger de Gaignières. On his death in 1716 the collection entered the Cabinet du Roi, precursor of the Bibliothèque Nationale. Gaignières seems to have had a particular preference for small sixteenth-century portraits and many now in the Louvre came originally from his collection. Some, which during the Revolution had passed into Alexandre Lenoir's Musée des Monuments Français, entered the Louvre in 1817; others were acquired later. In 1908 the Société des Amis du Louvre donated the highly important portrait of *Pierre Quthe* by François Clouet (p. 21). Of the more recent acquisitions that of Corneille de Lyon's *Pierre Aymeric* (p. 22) in 1976 is particularly significant as one of his few documented works. Also of note is the purchase in 1967 of the rare *Portrait of a couple* (p. 24). Thus the Louvre is able to exhibit a comprehensive collection of sixteenth-century portraits. Their precision and concern for the character of the sitter are derived from northern models, features which were to be the hallmarks of French portraiture, and continually developed in later centuries.

Taste for Mannerist art is more recent even than that for early portraits. The Italian artists who came to France in the sixteenth century gave rise to a complete change in taste, giving François I's court a style of painting that was elegant and decorative, very often with mythological settings. This charming Fontainebleau School, with its accent on the artificial, has only been studied during the past few decades and has only recently been represented in the Louvre. The famous *Diana, goddess of the hunt* (p. 19) was acquired for Fontainebleau during Louis-Philippe's reign because it was thought to be a portrait of Diane de Poitiers, Henri II's favourite. Apart from a few other exceptions—Gourmont's *Adoration of the shepherds*, the works by Dubreuil from the chapel of the Château d'Écouen and *The Last Judgement* by Cousin the Younger seized from the convent of the Minimes, Vincennes—the collection has been built up over the past sixty years. *Eva Prima Pandora* by Cousin the Elder (p. 18) was presented in 1922, the very popular *Gabrielle d'Estrées and one of her sisters* (p. 24) was purchased in 1937 and *Augustus and the Sybil* by Caron (p. 23) presented in 1958. Recently a great effort has been made to form a collection which will show all aspects of the Fontainebleau School, with purchases including the mid-sixteenth-century *Charity* (p. 19), in 1970, and in 1973 *The justice of Othon* attributed to Luca Penni.

SCHOOL OF PARIS, second half of the 14th century
The Narbonne altar-frontal, circa 1375
Black ink on silk   77.5 × 286 cm
Purchased in 1852

SCHOOL OF PARIS, second half of the 14th century
Jean II le Bon, King of France, circa 1360
Wood   59.8 × 44.6 cm
Extended loan from the Bibliothèque Nationale, 1925

9

JEAN MALOUEL
Niemegen, before 1370 – Dijon, 1415
Pietà known as '*La grande Pietà ronde*',
  circa 1400
Wood   diameter 64.5 cm
Purchased in 1864

JEAN DE BEAUMETZ
Artois, first known in 1361 – Dijon, 1396
Crucifixion with a Carthusian monk, between 1389 and 1395
Wood   60 × 48.5 cm
Purchased in 1967

SCHOOL OF PARIS OR BURGUNDY, early 15th century
The Entombment of Christ, circa 1400
Wood   32.8 × 21.3 cm
Purchased in 1869

10

HENRI BELLECHOSE
Brabant, known in Dijon from 1415 – Dijon, 1440/44
The St. Denis altar-piece, finished in 1416
Wood transferred to canvas   162 × 211 cm
Presented by Frédéric Reiset, 1863

Jean de Beaumetz, Jean Malouel and Henri Bellechose, working in Dijon, were successively the official artists of the Dukes of Burgundy, Philippe le Hardi and Jean sans Peur. The Louvre is extremely fortunate in possessing a painting by each of them. Characteristic of their work is the combination of refined draughtsmanship with fresh, brilliant colours heightened by gilding, in an attempt to express deep emotion.

JEAN FOUQUET
Tours, *circa* 1420 – Tours, 1477/81
Guillaume Jouvenel des Ursins, Chancellor of France, circa 1460
Wood   93 × 73.2 cm
Purchased in 1835

JEAN FOUQUET
Tours, *circa* 1420 – Tours, 1477/81
Charles VII, King of France, circa 1445(?)
Wood 85.7 × 70.6 cm
Purchased in 1838

JEAN HEY, called the Master of Moulins
Active in central France between 1480 and 1500
Charles-Orlant, Dauphin of France, 1494
Wood   28.5 × 23.5
Presented by Carlos de Beistegui, 1942

JEAN HEY, called the Master of Moulins
Active in central France between 1480
   and 1500
A donor and St. Mary Magdalen, circa 1490
Wood   56 × 40 cm
Purchased in 1904

FLEMISH ARTIST IN PARIS, mid–15th century
The Paris Parlement altar-piece, probably commissioned in 1452
Wood   226.5 × 270 cm
Seized during the French Revolution

Executed by a Flemish artist strongly influenced by the
work of Rogier van der Weyden, this altar-piece, still in its
original carved wood frame, shows the patrons of the
French monarchy (St. Louis, St. Denis, and Charlemagne)
grouped around the Crucifixion. In the background, on
the left-hand side, is a very accurate depiction of the
Louvre as it was in the middle of the fifteenth century.
Until the French Revolution the altar-piece hung in the
Chambre Dorée of the Paris Parlement and can be seen
there in Nicolas Lancret's painting of the Parlement
(see p. 61).

ENGUERRAND QUARTON
Active in Provence between 1444 and 1466
The Villeneuve-les-Avignon Pietà, circa 1455(?)
Wood 163 × 218.5 cm
Presented by the Société des Amis du Louvre, 1905

NICOLAS DIPRE
Active in Avignon from 1495 – Avignon, 1532
The Presentation of the Virgin, circa 1500
Wood 31.7 × 50 cm
Presented by Pierre Landry, 1972

One of the supreme examples of medieval painting, this
Pietà should now, after many years of discussion, be
recognised as a masterpiece by Quarton. The boldly
simplified and outlined forms, directness of treatment and
clarity of light are all characteristics of the School of
Provence in the fifteenth century. They are also found in
The Boulbon altar-piece and Dipre's *Presentation of the Virgin*;
and to a lesser extent in Lieferinxe's later *Crucifixion*.

PROVENÇAL ARTIST, mid–15th century
The Boulbon altar-piece, circa *1460*
Wood transferred to canvas   172 × 227.8 cm
Presented by the Committee for the exhibition of
    French primitive art, 1904

JOSSE LIEFERINXE, the Master of St. Sebastien
Hainaut, active in Provence from 1493 – Provence, 1505/08
The Crucifixion, circa 1500/05(?)
Wood   170 × 126 cm
Purchased in 1962

Attributed to Jean Clouet
?, 1485/90 – ?, 1540/41
François I, King of France, circa 1530(?)
Wood   96 × 74 cm
Collection of François I

JEAN COUSIN the Elder
Sens, *circa* 1490 – Paris, *circa* 1560
Eva Prima Pandora, circa 1550(?)
Wood   97.5 × 150 cm
Presented by the Société des Amis du Louvre, 1922

SCHOOL OF FONTAINEBLEAU, mid-16th century
Charity, circa 1560(?)
Canvas   147 × 96.5 cm
Purchased in 1970

SCHOOL OF FONTAINEBLEAU, mid-16th century
Diana, goddess of the hunt, circa 1550
Canvas   191 × 132 cm
Purchased in 1840

JEAN DE GOURMONT
Carquebut, *circa* 1483 – ?, after 1551
The Adoration of the shepherds, *circa* 1525(?)
Wood   93.5 × 115.5 cm
From the chapel of the Château d'Écouen

The setting of dreamlike architecture in this picture, clearly
inspired by Roman antiquity, although it is difficult to tell
whether it is under construction or in ruins, is given far
more prominence than the religious subject-matter.
Gourmont, who worked first in Paris and then in Lyons,
also executed engravings in which he often exploited his
virtuoso study of perspective.

FRANÇOIS CLOUET
? – Paris, 1572
Pierre Quthe, apothecary, 1562
Wood   91 × 70 cm
Presented by the Société des Amis du Louvre, 1908

FRANÇOIS CLOUET
? – Paris, 1572
Elisabeth of Austria, Queen of France, 1571(?)
Wood   36 × 26 cm
Collection of Louis XV; entered the Louvre in 1817

FRENCH ARTIST, second half of the 16th century
Portrait of a flautist with one eye, 1566
Wood   62 × 50 cm
Presented by Percy Moore Turner, 1948

CORNEILLE DE LYON
The Hague, *circa* 1500 – Lyons(?),
   circa 1575
Jean de Bourbon-Vendôme, circa 1550(?)
Wood   19 × 15.5 cm
Purchased in 1883

CORNEILLE DE LYON
The Hague, *circa* 1500 – Lyons(?),
   circa 1575
Pierre Aymeric, 1534
Wood   16.5 × 14.2 cm
Purchased in 1976

ANTOINE CARON
Beauvais, 1521 – Paris, 1599
Augustus and the Sybil, circa 1575/80
Canvas   125 × 170 cm
Presented by Gustave Lebel, 1938

Caron, who was Catherine de Médicis' official artist and
whose paintings often seem to echo the royal fêtes, shows
here the Emperor Augustus on his knees in front of the
Sybil, who gestures towards the Virgin and Child in the
heavens. The architectural setting, reminiscent of theatre
decor, shows the Seine and possibly certain monuments of
Paris modified by the artist's imagination on the right-
hand side.

23

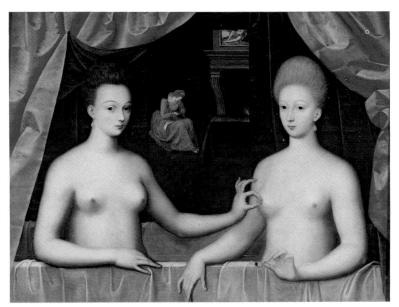

SCHOOL OF FONTAINEBLEAU, late 16th century
Gabrielle d'Estrées and one of her sisters, circa 1595(?)
Wood   96 × 125 cm
Purchased in 1937

TOUSSAINT DUBREUIL
Paris, *circa* 1561 – Paris, 1602
Hyante and Climène offering a sacrifice to Venus, circa 1600
Canvas 190 × 140 cm
From the Château Neuf, Saint-Germain-en-Laye

FRENCH ARTIST, early 17th century
Portrait of a couple, circa 1610(?)
Wood   73 × 96 cm
Purchased in 1967

The seventeenth century

The history of the Louvre's collection of seventeenth-century paintings illustrates changes in taste and the ways in which the rich and complex period has been valued. The collection, formed gradually by different contributions, first reflects the predilections of kings and then those of art historians.

Louis XIII acquired few works and the ones he owned came from vast pictorial schemes: the three allegorical figures by Vouet (p. 34), formerly part of the decoration of the Château Neuf, Saint-Germain-en-Laye, and two large works by Poussin from his Parisian period, *The institution of the Eucharist* (p. 38) commissioned in 1640 and also from Saint-Germain, and the ceiling painting *Truth carried off by Time* bequeathed by Cardinal Richelieu to the King with the Palais Cardinal, now the Palais Royal.

It was Louis XIV who, with unprecedented largesse, formed a magnificent collection of French art, a group of paintings which was essentially 'classical' in taste; a taste which could even be called 'Roman'—powerful and masculine, contrasting and often epic. In fact the collection chiefly consisted of works by three artists who were Roman by adoption, Poussin, Claude and Valentin, the only paintings considered worthy of being hung next to Italian sixteenth- and seventeenth-century masters, and of course it included paintings by the King's official artists, Le Brun and later Mignard. Thirty-one of the thirty-eight Poussins in the Louvre, a collection unrivalled anywhere in the world, belonged to Louis XIV. In 1665 he bought the Duc de Richelieu's thirteen famous canvases, amongst them *The four seasons* (p. 38), *Diogenes, Eliezer and Rebecca, The plague at Ashdod* (p. 36) and *The rescue of Pyrrhus.* Seven others were acquired in 1685, and in 1693 Le Nôtre gave the King *The adulterous woman, St. John baptising the people* and *The rescue of the infant Moses by Pharaoh's daughter.* Of the Louvre's works by Claude, ten came from Louis XIV, some were bought from the Duc de Richelieu, while others were given by Le Nôtre. Nearly all the Le Bruns, except those seized from churches during the French Revolution, and nearly all the Mignards also came to the Louvre from the King's collection. However, the collection was not confined only to these artists; works by a variety of other artists also feature in the 1710 inventory, among them *Charity* by Blanchard, *Acis and Galatea* by Perrier, *Augustus at Alexander's tomb* by Bourdon, and three by Stella, including *The Virgin and St. Anne* (now in Rouen) and *Minerva and the Muses* (p. 41).

Louis XV bought paintings that showed him to be heir to his great-grandfather's taste for solemn and heroic works. He bought Poussin's enormous *St. Francis Xavier* at the Jesuits' sale when their order was suppressed in 1763. At the same time Jean de Jullienne bought Vouet's *The Presentation in the Temple* (p. 35) which he gave to the Académie and which later entered the Louvre with the Académie's collection. The King also bought two fine Valentins from the estate of the Prince de Carignan in 1742.

Louis XVI, however, appreciated another aspect of seventeenth-century art, one that had previously been ignored by royal collectors. Contrary to the 'Roman' taste of Louis XIV, he and his Surintendant des Bâtiments, the Comte d'Angiviller, had what one might call 'Parisian' taste. Poussin was still appreciated, but as the King already had his ancestor's collection he concentrated on acquiring these more 'Parisian' works which were restrained, delicate and refined, with a predominance of clear, soft colours, not unlike the first works by eighteenth-century neo-classical artists such as Lagrenée. An artist who now became very popular was Eustache Le Sueur. In 1776 two large cycles by him entered the royal collection: twenty-two paintings depicting the life of St. Bruno painted for Chartreuse in Paris were given to the King by the monks at the instigation of the Comte d'Angiviller; whilst the decorative series from the Hôtel Lambert on the Île Saint-Louis, one from the Chambre des Muses (p. 47) and the other from the Cabinet de l'Amour were also acquired at this time. Louis XVI also bought Le Sueur's fine group portrait known as *A gathering of friends* (p. 46) and *Laban searching Jacob's baggage for the stolen idols* by La Hyre (p. 40).

Many paintings of similar 'Parisian' taste entered the collection during the French Revolution. Several were seized from the nobility: two small canvases by La Hyre from the Comte d'Angiviller, from the Duc de Penthièvre and the Duc d'Orléans two distinct and elegant Bourdons, and from the Quentin-Crawford collection two rare works by Stella. Also during the Revolution, Poussin's *Camillus and the schoolmaster of Falerii* was seized with the rest of the collection from the Galerie Dorée in the Duc de Penthièvre's Hôtel de Toulouse, and two little works by Claude were taken from the Duc de Brissac. Seizures from convents and churches constituted a major contribution: an enormous number of paintings, often of vast proportions, were thus added to the national collection, including nearly all the works by Philippe de Champaigne now in the Louvre and many masterpieces by Le Sueur, Bourdon, Le Brun and La Hyre. Despite this great influx of riches, paintings continued to be purchased, the government of the Directory buying Poussin's *Self-portrait* (p. 36) in 1797.

Very few contributions were made during the first half of the nineteenth century. However, Champaigne's masterpiece, *Portrait of a man* (p. 42) was purchased by Vivant Denon, Director of the Museum, in 1806 and another portrait by Champaigne was bought in 1835, a double portrait reputedly of Mansart and Perrault. *Apollo and Daphne*, Poussin's last painting, left unfinished at his death, was bought during the Second Empire; but it was not until 1911 that *The inspiration of the poet* (p. 37) entered the Louvre.

With the progressive rediscovery of a seventeenth century which could be termed 'realist' during the last half of the nineteenth century and the beginning of the twentieth, a new visual awareness reinstated 'painters of reality'. The seventeenth-century art of the La Caze collection was realist: besides the two large state portraits by Champaigne and a *'bambochade'* by Bourdon, there was above all *The peasant's meal* by Le Nain. Between 1869 and 1915 seven paintings by the Le Nain brothers entered the Louvre, including *The haywain* (p. 44) and *The peasant family* (p. 43). It was during these same years that mid-nineteenth-century artists such as Courbet, Millet and Rousseau, expounders of another kind of realism, began at last to appear in the

Louvre's collection. Twentieth-century keepers, who have continued to augment the series by the Le Nain brothers, added still lifes, absent until then, such as those by Baugin and Dupuis (p. 45), and formed the finest collection of paintings by Georges de La Tour in existence, notably the famous *Christ with St. Joseph* (p. 32). Acquisitions began in 1926 and continued progressively as La Tour's work was rediscovered. Recently the Louvre has been enhanced by the addition of two more famous canvases by him, *The cheat* (p. 32) from the Landry collection and *St. Sebastian tended by Irene* (p. 33), presented by the Société des Amis du Louvre, as well as two masterpieces by the Le Nain brothers, the delightful *Victory* and *The group of smokers* traditionally known as *The guard-room* (p. 44). The moving portrait of *Arnauld d'Andilly* in old age, painted by Champaigne at the end of his life, entered the collection in 1979 in lieu of death duties, and in 1980 the Société des Amis du Louvre, ever generous, presented Bourdon's lyrical *A subject from Roman history* (p. 46), filling a gap in the collection.

The Louvre now possesses a superb collection of seventeeth-century French painting with all its different facets represented. This will become even more apparent when the huge works by Champaigne, Le Sueur, Le Brun and Poussin, which have been confined to the reserve collection for so long, are finally exhibited. However, even with such a magnificent display there are a few gaps to be filled. For instance, the Louvre has no late work by Claude nor a major painting by La Hyre. Except for Valentin, the French followers of Caravaggio are poorly represented, despite two important recent acquisitions, *The young singer* (p. 30), one of the most successful pictures executed by Vignon during his stay in Rome and the huge and somewhat unadventurous *Prince Marcantonio Doria* painted by Vouet in Genoa (p. 34). The century also produced a large number of highly successful still life painters, who are meagrely represented in the Louvre's collection. Today some of these are perhaps considered second-rate, but opinions are constantly changing. At the beginning of this century few people had heard of Georges de La Tour.

VALENTIN DE BOULOGNE
Coulommiers, 1594 – Rome, 1632
Concert with Roman bas-relief, circa 1622/25
Canvas   173 × 214 cm
Collection of Louis XV, purchased in 1742

VALENTIN DE BOULOGNE
Coulommiers, 1594 – Rome, 1632
The judgement of Solomon, circa 1625(?)
Canvas   176 × 210 cm
Collection of Louis XIV, purchased in 1661

The influence of Caravaggio's dramatic style which
revolutionised European painting at the beginning of the
seventeenth century can be seen clearly in Valentin's work.
He would have come into contact with Caravaggio's work
in Rome where he went as a very young man, and spent all
of his short career. In *The judgement of Solomon* the strength
of forms outlined against the shadow, so reminiscent of
Caravaggio, does not preclude an atmosphere of mystery
and poetry that is peculiar to Valentin. Louis XIV owned
several of his paintings; five are still hanging in the King's
bedchamber in the Château de Versailles.

CLAUDE VIGNON
Tours, 1593 – Paris, 1670
The young singer, circa 1622/23
Canvas   95 × 90 cm
Presented by the Société des Amis du Louvre,
   1966

VALENTIN DE BOULOGNE
Coulommiers, 1594 – Rome, 1632
The fortune-teller, circa 1628
Canvas   125 × 175 cm
Collection of Louis XIV, purchased before 1683

CLAUDE VIGNON
Tours, 1593 – Paris, 1670
Solomon and the Queen of Sheba, 1624
Canvas   80 × 119 cm
Purchased in 1933

NICOLAS RÉGNIER
Maubeuge, 1591 – Venice, 1667
The fortune-teller, circa 1625
Canvas   127 × 150 cm
Purchased in 1816

GEORGES DE LA TOUR
Vic-sur-Seille, 1593 – Lunéville, 1652
The cheat, circa 1635(?)
Canvas   106 × 146 cm
Purchased in 1972

GEORGES DE LA TOUR
Vic-sur-Seille, 1593 – Lunéville, 1652
Christ with St. Joseph in the carpenter's shop, circa 1640(?)
Canvas   137 × 102 cm
Presented by Percy Moore Turner, 1948

GEORGES DE LA TOUR
Vic-sur-Seille, 1593 – Lunéville, 1652
The penitent Magdalen with night-light, called
The Terff Magdalen, circa 1640/45(?)
Canvas   128 × 94 cm
Purchased in 1949

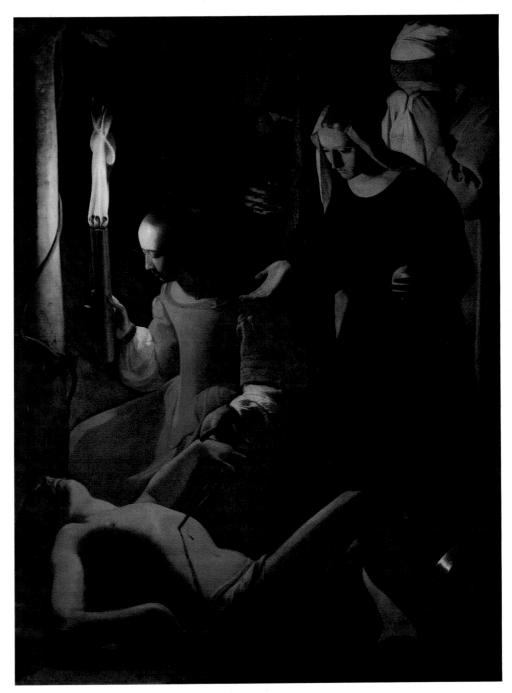

GEORGES DE LA TOUR
Vic-sur-Seille, 1593 – Lunéville, 1652
St. Sebastian tended by Irene, 1649(?)
Canvas   167 × 131 cm
Presented by the Société des Amis du Louvre, 1979

This painting was discovered in the church of Bois-Anzeray in 1945 and is almost certainly the canvas known to have been given by the town of Lunéville to La Ferté, governor of Lorraine at the end of 1649. It is the most complete and ambitious of La Tour's night scenes, with the blue of the coat reverberating in the range of warm tones, and is also one of his last works. An old copy of good quality is in the museum of Berlin-Dahlem.

SIMON VOUET
Paris, 1590 – Paris, 1649
Prince Marcantonio Doria, 1621
Canvas   129 × 95 cm
Anonymous gift, 1979

SIMON VOUET
Paris, 1590 – Paris, 1649
Allegory of wealth, *circa* 1630/35
Canvas   170 × 124 cm
Collection of Louis XIII

NICOLAS TOURNIER
Montbéliard, 1590 – Toulouse(?), 1638/39
Crucifixion with the Virgin, St. John and St. Vincent de Paul, *circa*
   1635(?)
Canvas   422 × 292 cm
Exchanged with the Musée de Toulouse in 1800

SIMON VOUET
Paris, 1590 – Paris, 1649
The Presentation in the Temple, 1641
Canvas   393 × 250 cm
From the main altar of the Jesuit church
now Saint Paul-Saint Louis, Paris
Collection of the Académie

NICOLAS POUSSIN
Les Andelys, 1594 – Rome, 1665
Self-portrait, 1650
Canvas   98 × 74 cm
Purchased in 1797

NICOLAS POUSSIN
Les Andelys, 1594 – Rome, 1665
The plague at Ashdod, 1630
Canvas   148 × 198 cm
Collection of Louis XIV, purchased in 1665

NICOLAS POUSSIN
Les Andelys, 1594 – Rome, 1665
Echo and Narcissus, circa 1628/30(?)
Canvas   74 × 100 cm
Collection of Louis XIV, purchased
   before 1683

NICOLAS POUSSIN
Les Andelys, 1594 – Rome, 1665
The inspiration of the poet, circa 1630(?)
Canvas   182.5 × 213 cm
Purchased in 1911

Poussin spent almost all his career in Rome painting in
isolation. He endeavoured to create a clear visual language
that would appeal to the spectator's mind and affect him
rationally rather than through the emotions. His oeuvre is
one of the supreme expressions of classicism in French art.
The subject of *The inspiration of the poet* remains under
discussion: it is possible that the young man on the right,
being inspired by Apollo, is Virgil and the figure standing
on the left Calliope, muse of epic poetry. In both figures
there are direct references to antique sculpture, as so often
in Poussin's work, and the golden light shows the influence
of the great Venetian painters of the sixteenth century.

NICOLAS POUSSIN
Les Andelys, 1594 – Rome, 1665
The institution of the Eucharist, 1640
Canvas   325 × 250 cm
Painted for the Sainte-Chapelle,
    Saint-Germain-en-Laye
Collection of Louis XIII

NICOLAS POUSSIN
Les Andelys, 1594 – Rome, 1665
Winter or *The Deluge*, between 1660 and
    1664
Canvas   118 × 160 cm
One of a series of four paintings
    depicting the seasons
Collection of Louis XIV, purchased in
    1665

CLAUDE GELLÉE, called LE LORRAIN
Chamagne, 1600 – Rome, 1682
The disembarkation of Cleopatra at Tarsus, circa
   1642/43
Canvas   119 × 170 cm
Collection of Louis XIV, purchased before 1683

CLAUDE GELLÉE, called LE LORRAIN
Chamagne, 1600 – Rome, 1682
Ulysses returns Chryseis to her father, 1648(?)
Canvas   119 × 150 cm
Collection of Louis XIV, purchased in 1665

CLAUDE GELLÉE, called LE LORRAIN
Chamagne, 1600 – Rome, 1682
Landscape with Paris and Oenone, called *The ford*,
1648
Canvas   119 × 150 cm
This painting is a pendant to *Ulysses returns*
Chryseis to her father above
Collection Louis XIV, purchased in 1665

39

JACQUES BLANCHARD
Paris, 1600 – Paris, 1638
Venus and the three Graces surprised by a mortal, circa 1631/33
Canvas   170 × 218 cm
Purchased in 1921

LAURENT DE LA HYRE
Paris, 1606 – Paris(?), 1656
Laban searching Jacob's baggage for the stolen idols, 1647
Canvas   95 × 133 cm
Collection of Louis XVI

FRANÇOIS PERRIER
Saint-Jean-de-Losne (?), *circa* 1600(?) – Paris, 1650
Aeneas and his companions fighting the Harpies, circa 1646/47
Canvas   155 × 218 cm
From the Cabinet de l'Amour in the Hôtel Lambert, Paris
Collection of Louis XVI, purchased in 1776

PIERRE PATEL the Elder
Picardy, *circa* 1605 – Paris, 1676
Landscape with ruins, circa 1646/47
Canvas   73 × 150 cm
From the Cabinet de l'Amour in the
    Hôtel Lambert, Paris.
Collection of Louis XVI, purchased in
    1776

JACQUES STELLA
Lyons, 1596 – Paris, 1657
Minerva and the Muses, circa 1640/50
Canvas   116 × 162 cm
Collection of Louis XIV

PHILIPPE DE CHAMPAIGNE
Brussels, 1602 – Paris, 1674
The miracles of the penitent St. Mary, 1656
Canvas   219 × 336 cm
From the apartments of Anne of Austria in the convent
    of Val de Grâce, Paris
Seized during the French Revolution

PHILIPPE DE CHAMPAIGNE
Brussels, 1602 – Paris, 1674
Portrait of a man, 1650
Canvas   91 × 72 cm
Purchased in 1906

PHILIPPE DE CHAMPAIGNE
Brussels, 1602 – Paris, 1674
The Ex-voto of 1662, 1662
Canvas   165 × 229 cm
Seized during the French Revolution

LOUIS or ANTOINE LE NAIN
Laon, *circa* 1600/10 – Paris, 1648
The peasant family, *circa* 1640/45
Canvas   113 × 159 cm
Purchased in 1915

The peasant family is the most monumental and moving of
the peasant subject paintings for which the Le Nain
brothers are renowned. There was no equivalent in
seventeenth-century European painting and the low-keyed
tones and careful attention given to the individuals were
not to be seen again until the nineteenth century in the
work of Realists such as Corot or Millet.

LOUIS or ANTOINE LE NAIN
Laon, *circa* 1600/10 – Paris, 1648
The haywain, also called *The return from
    hay-making*, 1641
Canvas   56 × 76 cm
Bequeathed by Vicomte Philippe de
    Saint-Albin, 1879

LOUIS or ANTOINE LE NAIN
Laon, *circa* 1600/10 – Paris, 1648
The group of smokers, also called *The
    guard-room*, 1643
Canvas   117 × 137 cm
Purchased in 1969

MATHIEU (?) LE NAIN
Laon, *circa* 1608/10 – Paris, 1677
The supper at Emmaus, circa 1645(?)
Canvas   75 × 92 cm
Purchased in 1950

LUBIN BAUGIN
Pithiviers, *circa* 1612 – Paris, 1663
Still life with wafer biscuits, circa 1630/35
Wood   41 × 52 cm
Purchased in 1954

PIERRE DUPUIS
Monfort l'Amaury, 1610 – Paris, 1682
Still life with basket of grapes, circa 1650(?)
Canvas   50 × 60 cm
Purchased in 1951

SÉBASTIEN BOURDON
Montpellier, 1616 – Paris, 1671
The beggars, circa 1635/40(?)
Wood   49 × 65 cm
Royal Collection

SÉBASTIEN BOURDON
Montpellier, 1616 – Paris, 1671
A scene from Roman history (Antony and Cleopatra?), circa 1645(?)
Canvas   145 × 197 cm
Presented by the Société des Amis du Louvre, 1979

EUSTACHE LE SUEUR
Paris, 1617 – Paris, 1655
Group portrait, called *A gathering of friends, circa* 1640/42
Canvas   127 × 195 cm
Collection of Louis XVI

EUSTACHE LE SUEUR
Paris, 1617 – Paris, 1655
Three muses: Melpomene, Erato and Polyhymnia,
circa 1652/55
Wood   130 × 130 cm
From the Chambre des Muses in the Hôtel
Lambert, Paris
Collection of Louis XVI, purchased in 1776

EUSTACHE LE SUEUR
Paris, 1617 – Paris, 1655
St. Gervase and St. Protase brought before Anastasius
for refusing to sacrifice to Jupiter, commissioned in
1652
Canvas   357 × 684 cm
Cartoon for the tapestry in Saint Gervais, Paris
Seized during the French Revolution

CHARLES LE BRUN
Paris, 1619 – Paris, 1690
Pietà, between 1643/45
Canvas   146 × 222 cm
Seized during the French Revolution

CHARLES LE BRUN
Paris, 1619 – Paris, 1690
Alexander and Porus, exhibited at the
   Salon of 1673
Canvas   470 × 1264 cm
Collection of Louis XIV

CHARLES LE BRUN
Paris, 1619 – Paris, 1690
Chancellor Séguier, circa 1655/57
Canvas 295 × 351 cm
Purchased in 1942, with the help of the
Société des Amis du Louvre

CHARLES LE BRUN
Paris, 1619 – Paris, 1690
The Adoration of the shepherds, 1689
Canvas   151 × 213 cm
Collection of Louis XIV

PIERRE MIGNARD
Troyes, 1612 – Paris, 1695
The Virgin of the grapes, *circa* 1640/50(?)
Canvas   121 × 94 cm
Collection of Louis XIV

The end of Louis XIV's reign and the Regency

It could seem somewhat arbitrary to group together artists from the end of Louis XIV's reign and those from his nephew's Regency. Rigaud's *Louis XIV* (p. 55) and Watteau's *Pilgrimage to Cythera* (p. 59) each seem to typify the mood of the century in which they were produced; the first by its ostentation and solemnity, the second by its refined and dreamy elegance, although only sixteen years separate them. For a long time French painting of around 1700 was deemed to be uninteresting, academic and too much influenced by the taste of the court. Now, after recent art historical research, and new evaluation of the work of Rubens and Titian, the variety and creativity of this period are appreciated, and it is interesting, despite the difference in generations, to consider La Fosse, Jouvenet, Coypel, Rigaud and Largillière with the younger Watteau and Lemoyne (both of whom died young), since all acknowledge their debt to the rich and supple execution of Flemish painters and the delightful colour ranges used by the Venetians.

Most of the decorative works commissioned by Louis XIV still adorn, or have now been returned to, the palaces for which they were executed but some works by Coypel, La Fosse and Desportes from the royal collection are now in the Louvre. Paintings depicting the King's victories by Van der Meulen (p. 53) or Parrocel (p. 53) were also part of the royal collection and are now in the Louvre, as is the portrait of the King by Rigaud, a symbol of the French monarchy. The canvas had been intended as a gift for Philip V of Spain, Louis XIV's grandson, but on seeing the painting the King liked it so much that he decided to keep it and had a replica made to send to Madrid. During Louis XV's reign the collection acquired other paintings, for example, Rigaud bequeathed his last work, *The Presentation in the Temple* (p. 56), which owes so much to Rembrandt, to the King. Louis XVI still bought Coypels, Van der Meulens and he bought one canvas by Louis de Boulogne. But by then the taste for works of Louis XIV's period and that of the Regency was out of fashion and it was not until the Revolution that new paintings came into the collection: three little works by Lemoyne seized from the nobility and above all the fine series of Jouvenet's work from Parisian churches. During the Restoration Rigaud's portrait of *Bossuet* and Jouvenet's portrait of *Dr. Raymond Finot* (p. 55) were purchased, the latter because it was thought to be of Fagon, Louis XIV's doctor.

With the Académie collection, which entered the Louvre during the Revolution, came a number of Académie election paintings, many of which are masterpieces: Rigaud's portrait of *Desjardins* executed in 1692 for his acceptance in 1700, Largillière's portrait of *Le Brun* (1686), Desportes' *Self portrait as a huntsman* (1699) (p. 57), Santerre's *Susanna bathing* and Pater's *Fête champêtre* (1728). But the most important of these was the *Pilgrimage to Cythera* (p. 59), Watteau's most popular painting and for a long time the only one by him in the Louvre. In the Académie's collection were other important paintings such as Rigaud's *Portrait of the artist's mother from two different angles* (p. 55) bequeathed to the Académie by the painter, and Jouvenet's *The Descent from the Cross* (p. 54).

Of very great importance to the Louvre was the bequest of the La Caze collection in 1869. Dr. Louis La Caze, a painter himself, was a keen collector of well-executed pictures with vigorous brushwork, and therefore favoured works from a period influenced by Titian, Rubens and Rembrandt. His taste can be seen in the *Democritus* by Antoine Coypel (p. 57) and in *Hercules and Omphale* by Lemoyne (p. 62). The breadth and quality of collections of works by certain artists in the Louvre is entirely due to the generosity of La Caze. For example, he bequeathed six works by Largillière, including the *Family portrait* (p. 57) originally thought to be of the artist himself and his family, and many works by Pater and Watteau. La Caze's eight Watteaus, including *The judgement of Paris* (p. 58) and *Gilles* (p. 60), which had belonged to Vivant Denon, Director of the Musée Napoléon, meant that this most poetic of French painters was at last fairly well represented in the Louvre.

Since then acquisitions of paintings from this period have been rare: a few works by Largillière have been given or bequeathed, a couple of theatre subjects by Gillot purchased in 1923 (p. 58) and in 1945, two rare silvery Lancrets, *The seat of justice* (p. 61) and *The decoration of the order of the Holy Spirit* were purchased in 1949, and a small Watteau landscape was presented in 1937. Recently two unusual works by Largillière have been acquired, a small landscape in 1971 and, in 1979, the theatrical *Decorative composition* (p. 56). But most importantly the group of Watteaus, despite La Caze, is still rather meagre, but has been augmented by the *Portrait of a gentleman* (p. 58) and *Diana bathing*.

Not until the opening of the new rooms will the true extent of the Louvre's rich collection of paintings from this period be appreciated. The huge, glowing religious compositions by Jouvenet, particularly *The miraculous draught of fishes* and *The resurrection of Lazarus* painted for Saint-Nicolas-des-Champs in Paris, will reveal an aspect of painting during Watteau's time that is not as yet well enough known.

CHARLES DE LA FOSSE
Paris, 1636 – Paris, 1716
The rescue of the infant Moses by Pharaoh's daughter,
commissioned in 1701
Canvas   125 × 110 cm
Collection of Louis XIV

ADAM FRANS VAN DER MEULEN
Brussels, 1632 – Paris, 1690
The defeat of the Spanish army near Bruges canal, 1667,
  circa 1670(?)
Canvas 50 × 80 cm
Collection of Louis XIV

JOSEPH PARROCEL
Brignoles, 1646 – Paris, 1704
The crossing of the Rhine by the army of
  Louis XIV, 1672, 1699
Canvas 234 × 164 cm
Collection of Louis XIV

53

JEAN JOUVENET
Rouen, 1644 – Paris, 1717
The Descent from the Cross, 1697
Canvas 424 × 312 cm
Collection of the Académie

This bold and vigorous painting, with its magnificent harmony of warm colours, foreshadows the most beautiful of the nineteenth-century Romantic paintings. Executed for the church of the Capuchins in the Place Louis-le-grand, Paris, it was donated to the Académie Royale de Peinture et de Sculpture in 1756. During the French Revolution it was acquired by the Louvre, as were all the other paintings which had belonged to the Académie.

HYACINTHE RIGAUD
Perpignan, 1659 – Paris, 1743
Portrait of the artist's mother from two different angles, 1695
Canvas   83 × 103 cm
Collection of the Académie

JEAN JOUVENET
Rouen, 1644 – Paris, 1717
Dr. Raymond Finot, exhibited at the
  Salon of 1704
Canvas   73 × 59 cm
Purchased in 1838

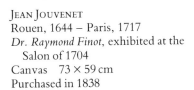

HYACINTHE RIGAUD
Perpignan, 1659 – Paris, 1743
Louis XIV, King of France, 1701
Canvas   277 × 194 cm
Collection of Louis XIV

ANTOINE COYPEL
Paris, 1661 – Paris, 1722
The swooning of Esther, exhibited at the Salon of 1704
Canvas   105 × 137 cm
Collection of Louis XIV

HYACINTHE RIGAUD
Perpignan, 1659 – Paris, 1743
The Presentation in the Temple, 1743
Wood   83 × 68 cm
Collection of Louis XV

NICOLAS DE LARGILLIÈRE
Paris, 1656 – Paris, 1746
Decorative composition, circa 1720/30(?)
Canvas   261 × 253 cm
Purchased in 1979

ANTOINE COYPEL
Paris, 1661 – Paris, 1722
Democritus, 1692
Canvas   69 × 57 cm
Bequeathed by Louis La Caze, 1869

NICOLAS DE LARGILLIÈRE
Paris, 1656 – Paris, 1746
Family portrait, circa 1710(?)
Canvas   149 × 200 cm
Bequeathed by Louis La Caze, 1869

JEAN-BAPTISTE SANTERRE
Magny-en-Vexin, 1658 – Paris, 1717
Susanna bathing, 1704
Canvas   205 × 145 cm
Collection of the Académie

FRANÇOIS DESPORTES
Champigneulles, 1661 – Paris, 1743
Self-portrait as a huntsman, 1699
Canvas   197 × 163 cm
Collection of the Académie

CLAUDE GILLOT
Langres, 1673 – Paris, 1722
The two coaches, circa 1710(?)
Canvas 127 × 160 cm
Purchased in 1923

JEAN ANTOINE WATTEAU
Valenciennes, 1684 – Nogent-sur-Marne, 1721
Portrait of a gentleman, circa 1715/20
Canvas 130 × 97 cm
Purchased in 1973

JEAN ANTOINE WATTEAU
Valenciennes, 1684 – Nogent-sur
  Marne, 1721
The judgement of Paris, circa 1720(?)
Wood 47 × 31 cm
Bequeathed by Louis La Caze, 1869

JEAN ANTOINE WATTEAU
Valenciennes, 1684 – Nogent-sur-Marne, 1721
The pilgrimage to Cythera, 1717
Canvas   129 × 194 cm
Collection of the Académie

It was with this painting, called at that time *The pilgrimage to Cythera*, that Watteau was officially accepted by the Académie Royale de Peinture et de Sculpture in 1717. The title *The departure for Cythera* under which it became famous is in fact incorrect as the pilgrims are already on the Island of Venus and are preparing to leave. The subject was inspired by Rubens' *Garden of love*. The open, curving composition, the clear colours and general mood of both happiness and nostalgia, were to be important influences on French eighteenth-century painting.

JEAN ANTOINE WATTEAU
Valenciennes, 1684 – Nogent-sur-Marne, 1721
Gilles, circa 1718/20(?)
Canvas   184.5 × 149.5 cm
Bequeathed by Louis La Caze, 1869

FRANÇOIS LEMOYNE
Paris, 1688 – Paris, 1737
The Assumption of the Virgin, circa 1731
Canvas   91.5 × 119 cm
Purchased in 1924

NICOLAS LANCRET
Paris, 1690 – Paris, 1743
*The seat of justice in the Parlement of
  Paris (1723), circa* 1724(?)
Canvas   56 × 81.5 cm
Purchased in 1949

JEAN–BAPTISTE PATER
Valenciennes, 1695 – Paris, 1736
The Chinese hunt, 1736
Canvas   55 × 46 cm
Presented by the Office des Biens Privés, 1950

FRANÇOIS LEMOYNE
Paris, 1688 – Paris, 1737
Hercules and Omphale, 1724
Canvas   184 × 149 cm
Bequeathed by Louis La Caze, 1869

The mid-eighteenth century

It is disappointing that Louis XV was not a keen collector, for during his reign sovereigns from the rest of Europe were voraciously buying contemporary French paintings: Frederick II of Prussia acquired the Watteaus, Lancrets and Chardins which today are the glory of Charlottenburg; his sister Louise-Ulrique of Sweden, well advised by her French ambassador Tessin, purchased the finest Bouchers and Chardins; Catherine the Great, Empress of Russia, bought the entire collection belonging to Louis-Antoine Crozat, Baron de Thiers, after his death in 1770. Comprising important paintings from all periods, the Crozat collection also included contemporary works. Louis XV, on the other hand, did not own a single painting by Watteau or Fragonard. He did, however, commission a number of paintings to hang over doors: still lifes from Chardin, such as the *Attributes of the Arts* and the *Attributes of Music* for the Château de Choisy, and from Lancret *The four seasons* for the Château de la Muette. For the Château de Fontainebleau he commissioned Van Loo's *The halt during the hunt* (p. 69) and Parrocel's *The halt of the grenadiers*. Many of the Bouchers, and the only Fragonard, *Chaereas and Callirrhoe* (p. 81), purchased during Louis XV's reign were tapestry cartoons and not easel paintings. Nevertheless, he did buy two of Chardin's most beautiful works at the Salon of 1740, *The diligent mother* (p. 72) and *Saying grace*. Also, the Marquis de Marigny, Surintendant des Bâtiments from 1751 to 1774, commissioned some large series which cannot be overlooked. One example of these is the group of fifteen large paintings depicting *The ports of France*, commissioned from Joseph Vernet in 1753 and completed in 1765. Today, except for the two in the Louvre (p. 78), this series is in the Musée de la Marine.

Louis XVI seems to have been scarcely more fond of contemporary painting than his grandfather but did purchase works by Subleyras, Carle Van Loo and Raoux, the most refined and restrained of eighteenth-century artists. He bought Greuze's already popular *The village bride* (p. 78) in 1782 at the sale following the death of the Marquis de Marigny, and commissioned Hubert Robert to paint the four large *Antiquities of France* (p. 84) for the Château de Fontainebleau.

Among works seized during the Revolution were six paintings by Subleyras from the Comte d'Angiviller, the Comte de Pestre Senef and the Duc de Penthièvre among others; and several landscapes by Joseph Vernet from the Comtesse du Barry, the Duchesse de Noailles and Boutin, Treasurer of the Navy. Two works by Vien and *The broken jug* by Greuze, one of his sentimental works which was highly regarded at the time, were also seized from the Comtesse du Barry. The Académie collection contained many important canvases of this period: election pieces by Boucher, *Renaud and Armide* (1734), Chardin, *The skate* and *The buffet* (p. 73), Tocqué, portraits of *Galloche* and *Lemoyne* (1734); portraits of *Oudry* and *Adam* (1753) by Perronneau and *Septimus Severus* (1769) by Greuze. Many works by Restout were taken from the churches and convents in Paris. A rare example of a French painting 'captured' abroad and subsequently left in the Louvre was Subleyras' vast *Christ in the house of Simon* which came from the convent of Asti near Turin to join the sketch for it which had been acquired by Louis XVI twelve years earlier. Subleyras (once again a 'Roman'), author of austere but delicate works, was one of the only painters from the first half of the eighteenth century to be appreciated during the neo-classical period (pp. 70 and 71). Not until the mid-nineteenth century was much interest taken in artists of Louis XV's reign, their work being considered frivolous and dissolute. Greuze, one aspect of whose work was serious and much concerned with virtue, was not scorned in quite the same way and the pair that complete *The father's curse, The ungrateful son* and *The punished son* (p. 79), were purchased in 1820.

The gift of Fragonard's *Music Lesson* in 1849 heralds a change in taste; *The inquisitive girls* by the same artist formed part of the Sauvageot gift in 1856. Chardin was now particularly appreciated and seven of his works were bought during the Second Empire, before the La Caze bequest, which was to form the major part of the Louvre's collection of mid-eighteenth-century French painting. With this bequest came the paintings that Louis XV and Louis XVI had not appreciated: thirteen major works by Chardin including *Still life with jar of olives* (p. 74), *The copper drinking fountain* (p. 74) and *The silver goblet*; nine sparkling Fragonards, among them *The bathers* (p. 83) and four imaginary figures; four Bouchers and several paintings by De Troy, Tocqué, Hubert Robert, Raoux, Nattier and Greuze. These beautiful works, which quickly became favourites with the public, were largely responsible for the general impression that the eighteenth century produced only small and charming paintings. La Caze's taste for these vigorous seductive works, canvases executed for collectors and avidly bought by them, even today tends to divert us from fully understanding the eighteenth century's ambitions towards '*la grande peinture*', paintings depicting subjects of morality and history.

The Louvre's collection continued to grow with purchases and bequests following on La Caze. Chardin's portraits of the Godefroy children, *Child with a top* and *Young man with a violin*, were purchased in 1907 and soon became popular; Boucher's *The afternoon meal* (p. 68) and the Louvre's most beautiful Nattier, *Comtesse Tessin* (p. 77), were bequeathed in 1895 by Dr. Achille Malécot; Chardin's *Portrait of Aved* (p. 72) was bequeathed by Paul Bureau in 1915; and several Greuzes were bequeathed by Baronne Nathaniel and Baron Arthur de Rothschild in 1899 and 1904. The bequest in 1915 of Baron Basile de Schlichting included works by Fragonard, Greuze, Nattier and Drouais.

Among more recent acquisitions the Carlos de Beistegui gift in 1942 contributed some important paintings: Fragonard's *Nude with cherubs* and an *Imaginary figure*; the most refined of Drouais, *Madame Drouais, wife of the artist* (p. 77); and a large work by Nattier, *The Duchesse de Chaulnes as Hébé*. The Sommier gift included Chardin's marvellous white and turquoise *The young draughtsman sharpening his pencil* (p. 75), the Péreire gift contained one of Vernet's most beautiful Italian scenes, *View of Naples*, which was later joined by its pair, another view of the same subject, and the Lyon gift (1961) contributed, amongst others, canvases by Robert and Vernet.

The most notable among recent acquisitions is the purchase of the famous *The bolt* (p. 83) one of the key pictures in Fragonard's late work.

More modest but nevertheless of great value are Subleyras' portrait of *Don Cesare Benvenuti* (p. 71), Delaporte's *Still life with a carafe of barley wine* (p. 74), and a youthful sketch by Boucher, which was bought in 1977, *Rebecca receiving Abraham's presents.* Among generous gifts should be mentioned the portrait of *Philippe Coypel* by his brother, Charles Antoine Coypel (p. 77) (Cailleux gift, 1968); Barbault's *The priest* and *The sultan* (François Heim gift, 1971); Dandré-Bardon's *Birth* (Benito Pardo gift, 1972); and Fragonard's *White bull* (Elaine and Michel David-Weill gift, 1976).

Thanks to the law which has been passed recently allowing the presentation of works of art in lieu of death duties, the Louvre's collection has gained three works which typify eighteenth-century France: Fragonard's portraits of the philosopher, *Diderot* (received in 1974) and the famous dancer, *Marie-Madeleine Guimard* (p. 82), and Chardin's *Still life with dead hare* (received in 1979). The policy of collecting views of the Louvre, which was originated by Hubert Robert, Director in the eighteenth century, should be mentioned. One painting was given by Maurice Fenaille in 1912, ten others have been purchased or given since 1946—interior and exterior, real and imaginary. The highlight of this project came in 1975 with the purchase of two large paintings that had been exhibited at the Salon of 1796, *Project for the redecoration of the Grande Galerie* and *Imaginary view of the Grande Galerie in ruins* (p. 84), both of which had for many years been in the Russian imperial collection in the palace of Tsarskoe-Selo.

Although pastels are not part of the collection of paintings in the Louvre but belong to the Department of Drawings, they should be mentioned because of their importance in French pictorial art as portraits 'painted in pastel'. The Louvre collection, unique both in number and quality, comes from the royal collection, the Académie collection and purchases and gifts during the nineteenth and twentieth centuries. The collections of works by Quentin de La Tour, Perronneau and Chardin, especially, are without equal.

Despite the fact that the Louvre's collection of paintings from the mid-eighteenth century rightly enjoys great prestige, there are nevertheless gaps that need to be filled. Few preliminary sketches, for example, which are one of the most attractive features of this period, have been acquired. However, it is important that, like that of the seventeenth century, eighteenth-century painting should be represented in all its different facets. The exhibition of the large canvases is a necessity which, with the opening of the new galleries in the Cour Carrée, will soon be realised. Only since 1968 has Fragonard's *Chaereas and Callirrhoe* been on view. At the beginning of this century one could see nearly all the French eighteenth-century paintings, small, medium or large, hung on thick material on three levels, frame touching frame, in the vast galleries which now display nineteenth-century art. Today such overcrowding would not be tolerated, but it is the Louvre's duty once again to exhibit the most important of the large paintings. Our entire vision of mid-eighteenth-century art could thus be changed.

FRANÇOIS BOUCHER
Paris, 1703 – Paris, 1770
Vulcan presenting Venus with arms for Aeneas, 1757
Canvas   320 × 320 cm
Tapestry cartoon for the Gobelins factory
Collection of Louis XV

This subject was often treated by Boucher, and the Louvre
has three other versions. The delightful and decorative
design, full of light and charm, was woven for the series of
tapestries *The loves of the gods*, and typifies the spirit of
Rococo decoration.

FRANÇOIS BOUCHER
Paris, 1703 – Paris, 1770
Diana bathing, 1742
Canvas   56 × 73 cm
Purchased in 1852

FRANÇOIS BOUCHER
Paris, 1703 – Paris, 1770
The forest, 1740
Canvas   131 × 163 cm
Presented by the Office des Biens
   Privés, 1951

FRANÇOIS BOUCHER
Paris, 1703 – Paris, 1770
The afternoon meal, 1739
Canvas   81.5 × 65.5 cm
Bequeathed by Dr. Achille Malécot, 1895

CARLE VAN LOO
Nice, 1705 – Paris, 1765
Aeneas carrying Anchises, 1729
Canvas   110 × 105 cm
Collection of Louis XVI

CARLE VAN LOO
Nice, 1705 – Paris, 1765
The halt during the hunt, 1737
Canvas   220 × 250 cm
Collection of Louis XV

JEAN-BAPTISTE OUDRY
Paris, 1686 – Beauvais, 1755
Still life with pheasant, 1753
Canvas   97 × 64 cm
Presented by the Office des Biens Privés, 1950

PIERRE SUBLEYRAS
Saint-Gilles-du-Gard, 1699 – Rome, 1749
Charon ferrying the Shades, circa 1735/40(?)
Canvas   135 × 83 cm
Seized during the French Revolution from the
collection of the Duc de Penthièvre

PIERRE SUBLEYRAS
Saint-Gilles-du-Gard, 1699 – Rome, 1749
Don Cesare Benvenuti , 1742
Canvas   138 × 101 cm
Purchased in 1969

JEAN SIMÉON CHARDIN
Paris, 1699 – Paris, 1779
*Portrait of the artist Jacques André Joseph
    Aved*, 1734
Canvas   138 × 105
Bequeathed by Paul Bureau, 1915

JEAN SIMÉON CHARDIN
Paris, 1699 – Paris, 1779
The diligent mother, exhibited at the Salon of 1740
Canvas   49 × 39 cm
Collection of Louis XV

It is said that Chardin began to paint interior scenes like
The diligent mother because he was annoyed by someone
saying that it was easy to paint still lifes. He based his art
on the Dutch tradition, revolutionising it completely by
his observation of reality and keen appreciation of colour
tones.

JEAN SIMÉON CHARDIN
Paris, 1699 – Paris, 1779
The buffet, 1728
Canvas   194 × 129 cm
Collection of the Académie

JEAN SIMÉON CHARDIN
Paris, 1699 – Paris, 1779
The copper drinking fountain, circa 1734
Wood   28.5 × 23 cm
Bequeathed by Louis La Caze, 1869

ROLAND DELAPORTE
Paris, 1724 – Paris, 1793
Still life with a carafe of barley wine, called '*La petite collation*', 1787
Canvas   37.5 × 46 cm
Purchased in 1979

JEAN SIMÉON CHARDIN
Paris, 1699 – Paris, 1779
Still life with jar of olives, 1760
Canvas   71 × 98 cm
Bequeathed by Louis La Caze, 1869

JEAN SIMÉON CHARDIN
Paris, 1699 – Paris, 1779
The young draughtsman sharpening his pencil, 1737
Canvas   80 × 65 cm
Presented by Madame Edmé Sommier, 1943

JEAN-BAPTISTE PERRONNEAU
Paris, 1715 – Amsterdam, 1783
Madame de Sorquainville, 1749
Canvas   101 × 81 cm
Presented by D. David Weill, 1937

FRANÇOIS-HUBERT DROUAIS
Paris, 1727 – Paris, 1775
Madame Drouais, wife of the artist,
circa 1758
Canvas   82.5 × 62 cm
Bequeathed by Carlos de
Beistegui, 1942

JEAN-MARC NATTIER
Paris, 1685 – Paris, 1766
Comtesse Tessin, 1741
Canvas   81 × 65 cm
Bequeathed by Dr. Achille Malécot,
1895

CHARLES-ANTOINE COYPEL
Paris, 1694 – Paris, 1752
Philippe Coypel, brother of the artist, 1732
Canvas   75 × 61 cm
Presented by Jean Cailleux and Denise
Cailleux, 1968

LOUIS TOCQUÉ
Paris, 1696 – Paris, 1772
Marie Leczinska, Queen of France, 1740
Canvas   277 × 191 cm
Collection of Louis XV

Joseph Vernet
Avignon, 1714 – Paris, 1789
View of Naples, 1748
Canvas 100 × 198 cm
Presented by André Péreire, 1949

Joseph Vernet
Avignon, 1714 – Paris, 1789
The town and harbour of Toulon, 1756
Canvas 165 × 263 cm
Collection of Louis xv

Jean-Baptiste Greuze
Tournus, 1725 – Paris, 1805
The village bride, exhibited at the Salon of 1761
Canvas 92 × 117 cm
Collection of Louis xvi, purchased in 1782

JEAN-BAPTISTE GREUZE
Tournus, 1725 – Paris, 1805
Self-portrait, circa 1785
Canvas   73 × 59 cm
Purchased in 1820

JEAN-BAPTISTE GREUZE
Tournus, 1725 – Paris, 1805
The punished son, 1778
Canvas   130 × 163 cm
Purchased in 1820

JOSEPH SIFFRED DUPLESSIS
Carpentras, 1725 – Versailles, 1802
Christophe Gabriel Allegrain, sculptor,
    1774
Canvas   130 × 97 cm
Collection of the Académie

NICOLAS BERNARD LÉPICIÉ
Paris, 1735 – Paris, 1784
The young draughtsman, Carle Vernet,
    aged fourteen, 1772
Canvas   41 × 33 cm
Bequeathed by Horace Paul Delaroche,
    1890

JEAN HONORÉ FRAGONARD
Grasse, 1732 – Paris, 1806
The storm, 1759(?)
Canvas   73 × 97 cm
Bequeathed by Louis La Caze, 1869

JEAN HONORÉ FRAGONARD
Grasse, 1732 – Paris, 1806
The high priest Chaereas sacrificing himself for Callirrhoe, 1765
Canvas   309 × 400 cm
Tapestry cartoon for the Gobelins factory (never executed)
Collection of Louis XV

It was thanks to this painting that Fragonard was accepted
by the Académie as a 'history painter'. He was soon to
abandon this type of subject-matter and devote himself to
the pleasant, often frivolous, paintings for which he is
famous. The movement in the composition, the sense of
drama and the strong light effects seen here are all in the
best tradition of Italian Baroque painting.

JEAN HONORÉ FRAGONARD
Grasse, 1732 – Paris, 1806
Marie-Madeleine Guimard, dancer, circa 1769
Canvas 81.5 × 65 cm
Presented in lieu of death duties, 1974

JEAN HONORÉ FRAGONARD
Grasse, 1732 – Paris, 1806
The bathers, circa 1772/75
Canvas   64 × 80 cm
Bequeathed by Louis La Caze, 1869

JEAN HONORÉ FRAGONARD
Grasse, 1732 – Paris, 1806
The bolt, circa 1778
Canvas   73 × 93 cm
Purchased in 1974

HUBERT ROBERT
Paris, 1733 – Paris, 1808
The Pont du Gard, exhibited at the Salon
    of 1787
Canvas   242 × 242 cm
Collection of Louis XVI

HUBERT ROBERT
Paris, 1733 – Paris, 1808
Imaginary view of the Grande Galerie in the
    Louvre in ruins, exhibited at the Salon
    of 1796
Canvas   114.5 × 146 cm
Purchased in 1975

The neo-classical period

Art historical research is again responsible for our ignoring traditional divisions by century, for the art of this period, which comprises the end of Louis XVI's reign, the Revolution and the Empire, has recently been re-assessed. Painting labelled 'neo-classical' was often thought to be cold and devoid of any true creativity, but recent exhibitions and publications have shown that it was, in fact, an extremely lively period, full of contradictions and rich in artistic personalities. French artists, above all Jacques Louis David, were the leaders of this European movement and no other museum can show the origins and development of neo-classical painting in France so comprehensively.

During Louis XVI's reign the policy of encouraging the painting of historical subjects, maintained by the Comte d'Angiviller, Surintendant des Bâtiments, meant that the King commissioned or purchased large paintings, often of Greek or Roman subjects destined to be woven as tapestries, several of which are still in the Louvre. The Direction des Bâtiments du Roi purchased two canvases by David which exploded upon the art scene and revolutionised painting of the period. These were *The oath of the Horatii* (p. 88) and *Brutus*, which stunned public and artists alike with their new plasticity and emotive power. At this time also Regnault's masterpiece of tortured elegance, *The Descent from the Cross* (p. 87), which had been commissioned as an altar-piece for the chapel at the Château de Fontainebleau, was purchased.

During the Revolution the government purchased a number of works that had been commissioned during the Monarchy, while paintings such as David's *Combat between Minerva and Mars* (second Prix de Rome in 1771) and Regnault's *Education of Achilles* (1782), were acquired with the Académie collection. Peyron's *The Funeral of Miltiades* (p. 87) and Madame Vigée-Lebrun's *Self-portrait with daughter* were among those seized from the Comte d'Angiviller, Gauffier's *Jacob and Laban's daughters* was seized from the Bernard collection, and David's signed copy of *Belisarius* from the Duchesse de Noailles.

During the Empire huge paintings of contemporary history were commissioned to glorify the Napoleonic era: David's *The Consecration of the Emperor Napoleon and Coronation of the Empress Josephine* (p. 91), and Gros' *Bonaparte visiting the plague-stricken at Jaffa* (p. 100) and *Napoleon on the battlefield of Eylau* (p. 99). The last two demonstrate the first important signs of the Romantic sensibility that was to pervade nineteenth-century Europe.

Nearly all the important acquisitions of '*la grande peinture*' of the neo-classical period came after the Restoration, when in 1818 the Musée de Luxembourg was created exclusively for the work of living artists and a deliberate acquisitions policy was established. Girodet's *The Deluge*, *The entombment of Atala* (p. 95) and *The sleep of Endymion* (p. 96) were bought in 1818, the large works by Guérin were bought between 1817 and 1830, except for *Phaedra and Hippolytus* which was bought at the Salon of 1802, Gérard's *Cupid and Psyche* (p. 96) was bought in 1822 and in 1826 Prud'hon's *Justice and Divine Vengeance pursuing Crime* (p. 94), executed for the Palais de Justice, was assigned to the Louvre by the City of Paris. In 1819 *The Sabine women* (p. 89) and *Leonidas at Thermopylae* were bought indirectly from David, by then in exile in Brussels. In 1823 the Comte d'Artois presented the painting of *Paris and Helen* that he had commissioned and purchased from David before the upheaval of the Revolution, and an unfinished masterpiece, the portrait of *Madame Récamier* (p. 90) was bought at the sale of David's studio in 1826, the year after his death.

In the second half of the nineteenth century portraits were the main contribution to the Louvre's collection of neo-classical art, often given or bequeathed by the artists' descendants, or by the sitters or their families. Two of Madame Vigée-Lebrun's masterpieces, another *Self-portrait* and the portrait of *Hubert Robert*, full of fire and tension (p. 90), were donated in 1843 by Madame Tripier-Le Franc, niece of the artist. David's portraits of *Monsieur Pécoul* and *Madame Pécoul* were acquired the next year and, in 1852, the artist Eugène Isabey presented a fine Gérard, the portrait of his father *Jean-Baptiste Isabey* (p. 97) and David's *Self-portrait*. In 1855 Madame Mongez bequeathed a double portrait by David of herself and her husband; David's *Madame Trudaine* (p. 90) was given in 1890 by Horace Paul Delaroche; and Gros' *Christine Boyer* (p. 99), Lucien Bonaparte's first wife, was acquired in 1894.

The twentieth century has added little to this exceptional collection, but the clear and fresh images of *Monsieur Sériziat* and *Madame Sériziat* by David were purchased in 1902. Acquisitions of note during this period are Prud'hon's *Young Zephyr* in the Schlichting bequest of 1915, David's only landscape, the exquisite *View of the Luxembourg gardens*, a gift of Bernheim-Jeune in 1912, and above all the Comte d'Espine's splendid collection given by his daughter, the Princesse de Croy, in 1930. The main feature of this collection was the group of landscapes painted in the open air by Michallon (27 works) and, more importantly, by Valenciennes (127 works) (p. 93). In the last fifty years more fine portraits have been acquired: *Madame de Verninac*, *Monsieur Meyer* and *General Bonaparte* by David; *Madame Lecerf* by Gérard and *Madame Pasteur* by Gros. In order to represent the whole range of neo-classical art a number of purchases in different areas have been made recently: Guérin's *The shepherds at Amyntas' tomb*, Regnault's *Socrates and Alcibiades* and the subtle *Still life with flowers* by the Lyonnais artist, Berjon.

This aim of covering the whole period in depth should remain paramount. Apart from the acknowledged masters whose works abound in the Louvre, many appealing artists, some only recently rediscovered, are scarcely represented if at all. The Louvre collection is undoubtedly without rival, and what needs to be done now is to give it the finishing touches and to represent the neo-classical period as completely as possible, showing all its many nuances.

JEAN-BAPTISTE REGNAULT
Paris, 1754 – Paris, 1829
The Descent from the Cross, 1789
Canvas 425 × 233 cm
Commissioned for the chapel in the
Château de Fontainebleau

JEAN-FRANÇOIS-PIERRE PEYRON
Aix-en-Provence, 1744 – Paris, 1814
The funeral of Miltiades, 1782
Canvas 98 × 136 cm
Seized during the French Revolution
from the collection of the Comte
d'Angiviller

JACQUES LOUIS DAVID
Paris, 1748 – Brussels, 1825
The oath of the Horatii, 1784
Canvas   330 × 425 cm
Collection of Louis XVI

Executed in Rome, this canvas was enthusiastically received when it was exhibited at the Paris Salon of 1785. Like Caravaggio's depictions of scenes from the life of St. Matthew before, and Picasso's *Demoiselles d'Avignon* after, *The oath of the Horatii* was to prove one of the great turning-points in the history of art. The sober realism, rigorous simplification of form and heroic tone of the subject-matter were all to be of significant influence on painting in the future.

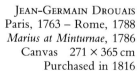
Jacques Louis David
Paris, 1748 – Brussels, 1825
The Sabine women, 1799
Canvas 385 × 522 cm
Purchased in 1819

Jean-Germain Drouais
Paris, 1763 – Rome, 1788
Marius at Minturnae, 1786
Canvas 271 × 365 cm
Purchased in 1816

ELISABETH LOUISE VIGÉE-LEBRUN
Paris, 1755 – Paris, 1842
Hubert Robert, artist, 1788
Wood   105 × 84 cm
Presented by Madame Tripier le Franc, 1843

JACQUES LOUIS DAVID
Paris, 1748 – Brussels, 1825
Madame Trudaine, circa 1792(?)
Canvas   130 × 98 cm
Bequeathed by Horace Paul Delaroche, 1890

JACQUES LOUIS DAVID
Paris, 1748 – Brussels, 1825
Madame Récamier, 1800
Canvas   174 × 244 cm
Purchased in 1826

JACQUES LOUIS DAVID
Paris, 1748 – Brussels, 1825
The Consecration of the Emperor Napoleon and Coronation of the Empress Josephine, 2nd December 1804, 1806/7
Canvas 621 × 979 cm
Commissioned by Napoleon I

By judicious grouping of the figures and clear lighting, David has avoided the muddle and confusion that could have resulted from the depiction of such a huge crowd. The consecration took place in the Cathedral of Notre Dame, Paris, in the presence of Pope Pius VII. Although the painting contains many individual realistic portraits, it also achieves a general feeling of dignity and grandeur. David could well have based the composition on that of Rubens' *The coronation of Marie de Médicis*, originally in the Palais du Luxembourg and now in the Louvre.

MARIE-GUILLEMINE BENOIST
Paris, 1768 – Paris, 1826
Portrait of a negress, exhibited at the Salon of 1800
Canvas   81 × 65 cm
Purchased in 1818

ANTOINE BERJON
Lyons, 1754 – Lyons, 1843
Still life with a basket of flowers, 1814
Canvas   66 × 50 cm
Purchased in 1974

LOUIS LÉOPOLD BOILLY
La Bassée, 1761 – Paris, 1845
Meeting of artists in Isabey's studio,
   exhibited at the Salon of 1798
Canvas   71.5 × 111 cm
Bequeathed by Monsieur Biesta-Monrival, 1901

PIERRE HENRI DE VALENCIENNES
Toulouse, 1750 – Paris, 1819
Storm at the edge of a lake, circa 1782/84
Paper on cardboard   39.8 × 52 cm
Collection of Comte de l'Espine;
presented by Princesse Louis de Croy,
1930

JOSEPH BIDAULD
Carpentras, 1758 – Montmorency, 1846
Landscape in Italy, 1793
Canvas   113 × 144 cm
Purchased at the Salon of 1793

PIERRE-PAUL PRUD'HON
Cluny, 1758 – Paris, 1823
The Empress Josephine, 1805
Canvas   244 × 179 cm
Collection of Napoleon III; presented in 1879

PIERRE-PAUL PRUD'HON
Cluny, 1758 – Paris, 1823
Justice and Divine Vengeance pursuing Crime, 1808
Canvas   244 × 294 cm
Commissioned for the Palais de Justice, Paris, and
    exchanged with the City of Paris in 1826

ANNE-LOUIS GIRODET DE ROUCY-TRIOSON
Montargis, 1767 – Paris, 1824
The entombment of Atala, 1808
Canvas   207 × 267 cm
Purchased in 1818

Atala, or the love of two savages in the desert, was published by
Chateaubriand in 1801 and inspired several painters. They
were seduced by the exotic subject-matter—the story of
the hopeless love of an Indian maiden, Atala, for a fellow
Indian, Chactas, set in Louisiana in the eighteenth century.
The tender and melancholy feeling in the painting and the
importance given to the contrast of light and shade,
diametrically opposed to David's style, is indicative of a
'pre-Romantic' sensibility, often one of the most attractive
aspects of painting during the neo-classical period. In an
even more dramatic and heightened manner, Prud'hon's
moonlit *Justice and Divine Vengeance pursuing Crime* shows
the same preoccupations, also very much 'anti-David'.

FRANÇOIS GÉRARD
Rome, 1770 – Paris, 1837
Cupid and Psyche, 1798
Canvas   186 × 132 cm
Purchased in 1822

ANNE-LOUIS GIRODET DE ROUCY-TRIOSON
Montargis, 1767 – Paris, 1824
The sleep of Endymion, 1793
Canvas   198 × 261 cm
Purchased in 1818

FRANÇOIS GÉRARD
Rome, 1770 – Paris, 1837
Jean-Baptiste Isabey, miniaturist, with his daughter, 1795
Canvas   194.5 × 130 cm
Presented by Eugène Isabey, 1852

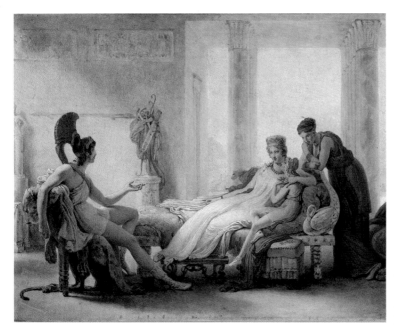

PIERRE-NARCISSE GUÉRIN
Paris, 1774 – Rome, 1833
Dido and Aeneas, sketch, 1815 or just before
Canvas   35 × 45 cm
Bequeathed by Adrien-Aimé Destouches, 1891

PIERRE-NARCISSE GUÉRIN
Paris, 1774 – Rome, 1833
The return of Marcus Sextus, 1799
Canvas   217 × 243 cm
Purchased in 1830

ANTOINE-JEAN GROS
Paris, 1771 – Meudon, 1835
Christine Boyer, circa 1800
Canvas 214 × 134 cm
Purchased in 1894

ANTOINE-JEAN GROS
Paris, 1771 – Meudon, 1835
Napoleon Bonaparte on the battlefield of Eylau, 1807, 1808
Canvas 521 × 784 cm
Commissioned after an open competition in 1807

Antoine-Jean Gros
Paris, 1771 – Meudon, 1835
Napoleon Bonaparte visiting the plague-stricken at Jaffa, 1799,
   1804
Canvas   523 × 715 cm
Commissioned by the State

This vast scene, full of warmth and lyricism, is a good
example of the interest in the Orient instigated by
Napoleon's battle campaigns. The subject-matter is
actually little more than political propaganda, but its
execution and the strong emotional appeal achieved by the
simple treatment of the victims' fevered rapture, renders
this canvas the first great success of Romanticism in
painting.

The nineteenth century

During the reigns of Louis XVIII and Charles X the collection acquired several masterpieces by living artists purchased directly from the Salon. These included Ingres' *Roger and Angelica* 1819, Delacroix's *Dante and Virgil* and *The massacre at Chios* (p. 114), in 1822 and 1824 respectively, and the huge canvases by Delaroche, Devéria and Scheffer in 1828. The royal administration had a reputation for banal and conventional taste, but these acquisitions show that it was not necessarily always bad. In fact it could even be courageous, as in the famous purchase of the scandalous *The raft of the Medusa* by Géricault (p. 111), the subject of which was a contemporary event exploited by the Opposition to fight the existing régime. The canvas, purchased by Dedreux-Dorcy at the artist's posthumous sale in 1824, was sold the following year to the Museum for its original price. All contemporary paintings were exhibited in the Musée du Luxembourg, which opened as the 'Galerie royale du Luxembourg' in 1818 exclusively for the works of living artists. They were not hung in the Louvre until later.

A major contribution to the Louvre during the Restoration in terms of contemporary art was not in the field of easel painting but in that of decoration. Ambitious designs for the Museum's new galleries have left the building with an impressive series of huge painted ceilings which are perhaps still not sufficiently studied. Of particular beauty are the two parallel series of rooms along the first floor of the south wing of the Cour Carrée, which today is still known as the Musée Charles X and houses the collections of Greek, Roman and Egyptian art. The ceilings of the Conseil d'État in the west wing of the Cour Carrée (now the Department of Objets d'Art) were also painted at this time, as were those rooms near the principal staircases of the Louvre (Salle Percier et Fontaine, and Salle Duchâtel). Thus many history painters, sometimes more conscientious than inspired, but in whom interest is now once again being revived, are represented permanently in the Louvre by their most ambitious works without the Museum having to purchase them or extract them from the reserve collections. Involved in this massive decorative scheme were not only ordinary artists such as Blondel, Picot, Alaux, M.M. Drolling and Mauzaisse, but also good painters such as Meynier, Heim, Schnetz, Abel de Pujol and Couder and true innovators such as E. Devéria, A.E. Fragonard (son of Jean-Honoré), L. Cogniet and H. Vernet (grandson of Claude-Joseph). Neither should the last and possibly less accomplished works by the brilliant Baron Gros be forgotten, nor one of Ingres' most elaborate compositions (p. 108), *The apotheosis of Homer*. This last-mentioned work was removed during the artist's lifetime and transformed into an easel painting for the Exposition Universelle of 1855 and was replaced by a copy painted by the Balze brothers.

During Louis-Philippe's reign the most important scheme was the Musée historique in the Château de Versailles, and the major commissions during this period were always destined for Versailles. The project was executed on a hitherto unprecedented scale which involved not only the decoration of a museum as had just been done at the Louvre under masterpieces, amongst them *The wounded man*, were bought at the sale of his studio in 1881. In that same year Juliette Courbet presented *The burial at Ornans*, one of her brother's most important canvases. Since December 1986 this, together with the other Courbets, has been housed in the Musée d'Orsay. The Millet canvases too are now on display there. Several of Millet's works were acquired at his posthumous sale in 1875; Madame Hartmann gave *Spring* in 1887 and Madame Pommery *The gleaners* in 1890. It was also after Ingres' death that several of his masterpieces came into the collection: among bequests were the three portraits of the Rivière family (p. 105) by Monsieur and Madame Rivière's daughter-in-law in 1870; *Oedipus* and *The spring* bequeathed by the Comtesse Ducharel in 1878; and *Cordier* by Comtesse Mortier in 1886. Purchases included the portrait of *Monsieur Bochet* in 1878, the *Valpinçon bather* (p. 107) in 1879, the famous *Monsieur Bertin* (p. 107) and *The 'grande odalisque'* (p. 106) in 1899. The series was crowned by the Société des Amis du Louvre's gift of *The Turkish bath* (p. 106) in 1911.

Three large gifts in the early years of this century meant that big collections of small or medium-sized paintings entered the Louvre and ensured magnificent representation of artists such as Corot, Delacroix, Decamps, Millet and the Barbizon School of landscape painters. In 1902, Thomy Thiéry, an Englishman of French origin from Mauritius living in Paris, bequeathed a collection consisting entirely of nineteenth-century paintings, among them Delacroix's *Medea, The abduction of Rebecca*, nine small canvases and many splendid Corots and Barbizon paintings. This collection, which has remained together, is still on display at the Louvre following the opening of the Musée d'Orsay. Even richer and more varied was the collection given by Étienne Moreau-Nélaton in 1906. It comprised no less than thirty-seven superbly selected Corots and several masterpieces by Delacroix, including *Still life with a lobster* and *Young girl in the graveyard*, as well as a sketch by Géricault for *The raft of the Medusa*. The Moreau-Nélaton collection included the most avant-garde and truly innovative of contemporary art and it was through this collection that the Louvre acquired several Manet's, including the well-known *Déjeuner sur l'herbe*, a series of exquisite landscapes by Claude Monet and paintings by Berthe Morisot, Sisley and Pissarro. The whole collection was exhibited in the Musée des Arts Décoratifs for a long time and did not enter the Louvre until 1934. Its Impressionist paintings, after having been exhibited in the Musée du Jeu de Paume, are now housed in the Musée d'Orsay. The third gift (1909), which is today exhibited in its entirety in the Musée d'Orsay, was made by Alfred Chauchard in 1909, a fine collection of works by Corot, Delacroix, Millet, Diaz, Decamps, Dupré, Daubigny and Meissonier often acquired at high prices. The sum of 800,000 francs paid by Chauchard in 1889 for Millet's *Angelus* caused a sensation at the time. The Camondo bequest in 1911 also included fine Delacroixs and Corots, as well as splendid Impressionists.

After the First World War the Louvre made several spectacular acquisitions in the field of nineteenth-century art. Courbet's masterpiece, *The artist's studio*, which is today exhibited, along with the other Courbet's, in the Musée d'Orsay, was purchased in 1920 with the help of both a public subscription and the Société des Amis du Louvre, and Delacroix's *The death of Sardanapalus* (p. 115), one of the greatest expressions of Romantic art, was purchased the following year. The generosity of owners, descendants of great artists, keen to see their forebears' oeuvre well represented in the Louvre, or of private collectors, has continued to this day. In the first category, Baron Arthur Chassériau should be mentioned above all. His fine gift in 1918 and bequest in 1933/34 amounted to forty-three canvases by his uncle showing the whole range of that artist's genius (p. 109). During the Charles X, but the formation of an entire collection of exhibits at the same time, all with a pomp not seen since the time of Louis XIV. The Galérie des Batailles alone is a matter for wonder. In 1885 the Louvre acquired Delacroix's *The entry of the Crusaders into Constantinople* from the museum in Versailles and this unforgettable canvas, full of melancholy and passion, is a fitting echo of Veronese's and Rubens' great works hanging nearby.

The most beautiful Delacroixs continued to be purchased at the Salon: *The women of Algiers* (p. 116) in 1834, and *The Jewish wedding* in 1841. His masterpiece, *Liberty guiding the people* (p. 115), one of the most glorious paintings in the Louvre, had been purchased by Louis-Philippe in 1831. However, the influence of the painting's message was so feared by the Government that it was only exhibited for a few weeks in the Musée du Luxembourg. It was then returned to Delacroix and remained hidden except for a brief time in 1849. It was later shown at the Exposition Universelle of 1855, was exhibited at the Musée du Luxembourg again from 1861 and finally reached the Louvre in 1874. Paradoxically, Delacroix's great rival, Ingres, despite being a classical painter and ardent follower of Raphael, was much less well treated by the State, who bought few of his works; the scandalous and revolutionary Delacroix, prime exponent of Romantic art, fared much better. Ingres' portrait of *Cherubini* was purchased in 1842, and he was commissioned to paint *The Virgin with Eucharistic wafer*, which he did not complete until 1854. Louis-Philippe's major contribution to the Louvre's collection of works by Ingres was the fascinating series of twenty-five cartoons for the stained glass windows in the chapels of Saint-Ferdinand de Paris and Saint-Louis de Dreux executed between 1842 and 1844. Couture's *The Romans of the decadence*, commissioned by the State, was purchased in 1847.

The brief but generous Republic of 1848 purchased works by Géricault, five in 1849, and the vast, sublime images of *The officer of the Imperial Guard charging* and *The wounded officer of the Imperial Guard leaving the battlefield* (p. 110) at the sale of Louis-Philippe's possessions in 1851, as well as commissioning Duban to execute the restoration of the Galerie d'Apollon. The painted decoration was not completed and the central panel of the vaulted ceiling was painted by Delacroix between 1850 and 1851 with a scene depicting *Apollo vanquishing the Python* (p. 117). Full of innovative lyricism, it is also magnificently in keeping with the paintings by Le Brun and eighteenth-century masters which surround it.

The acquisitions policy of the Second Empire was eclectic. Works by Delauny, Baudry, Carolus-Duran, Gérôme, Lenepveu, Meissonier and other good academic artists, which are today exhibited in the Musée d'Orsay, were purchased. Also, more adventurously, two Corots were acquired, *The dance of the nymphs* in 1851 and the famous *Souvenir de*

Mortefontaine (p. 120) at the Salon of 1864. Several works of Chassériau, Daubigny, Decamps and Rousseau were bought, and Gustave Moreau's *Orpheus* entered the Musée du Luxembourg in 1867. However, works of the great contemporary innovators of the Realist movement, who rejected official academic teaching, were not allowed into the Museum. Neither Millet, Courbet, Daumier, Troyon nor Dupré were exhibited.

Not until the end of the century, and after the artists' deaths, was this injustice rectified. Courbet's *The wave* was purchased in 1878, and many same period, between 1926 and 1932, the joint action of the Société des Amis du Louvre and the Société Chassériau ensured that the damaged paintings from the staircase in the Cour des Comptes, burnt in 1871, should be saved and preserved in the Louvre.

Recently private collectors have been particularly generous. In 1942 Carlos de Beistegui presented Ingres' portraits of *Bartolini* and *Madame Panckoucke*, and two small works by Meissonier, of which one was *The barricade*; in 1965 Baronne Gourgaud gave works by Corot and two splendid works by Delacroix and Daumier; James N.B. Hill gave, in 1962 and bequeathed in 1978, paintings by Troyon, Corot and Millet; and portraits of *Pierre-Joseph Proudhon* and *Madame Proudhon* by Courbet were presented by their grand-daughters in 1958. Two other fine works by Courbet, *Still life with trout* and *Nude figure with dog* have recently been received in lieu of death duties (1978 and 1979). In 1979 the Louvre's dazzling collection of works by Delacroix was augmented by the landscape it still needed, *The sea from the cliffs at Dieppe* (p. 116), an extraordinary painting like a Claude Monet view from the hand of Titian.

As the vast sphere of nineteenth-century art still has many scantly-explored areas, it is difficult to form a clear idea of exactly what the Louvre should exhibit in order to give an accurate impression of the century and to emphasise its particular innovations. The Louvre, of course, favours the acknowledged masters, and is apt to mirror the taste of late nineteenth-century collectors. However, there is now room for greater variety in the collection and a more comprehensive coverage of the period, for yet again taste has changed.

The creation of the Musée d'Orsay, which is devoted to the art of the second half of the nineteenth century, has fundamentally altered the balance of the collections of nineteenth-century French painting in the Louvre. Courbet, Millet, Daumier, the landscape painters of the Barbizon school have crossed the Seine, along with Puvis de Chavannes, Moreau, Couture, Meisonnier and the academic painters. Some canvases from the end of the careers of Ingres, Delacroix, Chassériau and Corot, essential to an appreciation of the painting of the Second Empire, have also been transferred to the Musée d'Orsay. However, the masterpieces of these artists, even their late works, have remained in the Louvre, so that their full careers can be traced: the *Turkish bath* by Ingres, the paintings of the Cour des Comptes by Chassériau, Corot's *Woman in blue* and *Bell tower of Douai*. Thus the bulk of the canvases from the first half of the nineteenth century can still be compared with the major works of earlier centuries. The opening of the Musée d'Orsay has provided an opportunity to cast a fresh eye over the painting of the second quarter of the nineteenth century, and to enrich the Museum's collections of this period; this policy has already led to the acquisition of canvases by Chassériau, Flandrin, Dubufe, Alexandre-Evariste Fragonard and Hesse.

JEAN AUGUSTE DOMINIQUE INGRES
Montauban, 1780 – Paris, 1867
Mademoiselle Rivière, exhibited at the Salon of 1806
Canvas   100 × 70 cm
Bequeathed by Madame Rivière, 1870

JEAN AUGUSTE DOMINIQUE INGRES
Montauban, 1780 – Paris, 1867
The Turkish bath, 1862
Canvas on wood   diameter 108 cm
Presented by the Société des Amis du Louvre, 1911

JEAN AUGUSTE DOMINIQUE INGRES
Montauban, 1780 – Paris, 1867
The 'grand odalisque', 1814
Canvas   91 × 162 cm
Purchased in 1899

The female nude was a subject that interested Ingres all his life. *The Turkish bath*, the last of his many variations on the theme, shows, as does *The 'grande odalisque'*, the fascination exerted by the Orient throughout the nineteenth-century. The *Valpinçon Bather* is a youthful work, painted whilst Ingres was staying at the Villa Medici. He was subsequently to return several times to this motif of a nude seen from behind, most notably fifty-four years later in *The Turkish bath*.

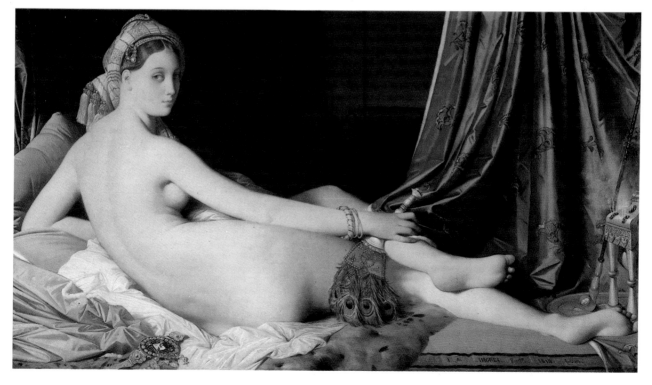

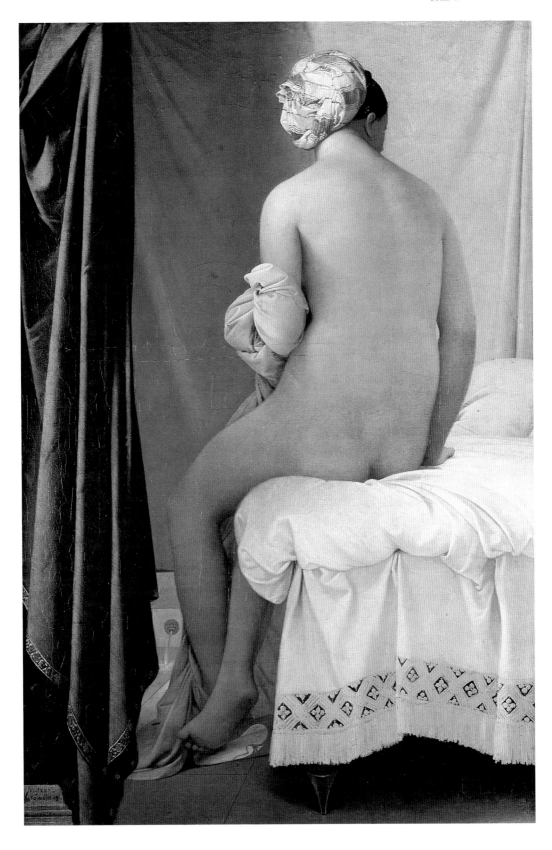

Jean Auguste Dominique Ingres
Montaubon, 1780 – Paris, 1867
The bather, known as *The Valpinçon bather*, 1908
Canvas 146 × 97 cm
Purchased in 1879

Jean Auguste Dominique Ingres
Montauban, 1780 – Paris, 1867
Monsieur Bertin, 1832
Canvas   116 × 95 cm
Purchased in 1897

Jean Auguste Dominique Ingres
Montauban, 1780 – Paris, 1867
The apotheosis of Homer, 1827
Canvas   386 × 512 cm
Originally a ceiling painting in the Salle Clarac in the Louvre,
  commissioned in 1826

THÉODORE CHASSÉRIAU
Sainte-Barbe-de-Samana, 1819 – Paris, 1856
The two sisters (the artist's sisters), 1843
Canvas   180 × 135 cm
Bequeathed by Baron and Baronne Arthur Chassériau, 1918

THÉODORE CHASSÉRIAU
Sainte-Barbe-de-Samana, 1819 – Paris, 1856
The toilet of Esther, 1841
Canvas   45.5 × 35.5 cm
Bequeathed by Baron Arthur Chassériau, 1934

THÉODORE CHASSÉRIAU
Sainte-Barbe-de-Samana, 1819 –
Paris, 1856
Peace, between 1844 and 1848
Canvas   340 × 362 cm
Fragment from the decoration of
the building of the Cour des
Comptes, burnt in 1871
Bequeathed by the Chassériau
Committee, 1903

THÉODORE GÉRICAULT
Rouen, 1781 – Paris, 1824
The wounded officer of the Imperial Guard leaving the battlefield,
  exhibited at the Salon of 1814
Canvas   358 × 294 cm
Purchased in 1851

THÉODORE GÉRICAULT
Rouen, 1781 – Paris, 1824
The raft of the Medusa, exhibited at the Salon of 1819
Canvas 491 × 716 cm
Purchased in 1824

This painting was a '*succès de scandale*' at the Salon of 1819, recalling the wreck of the *Medusa* in 1816 and the shameful inability of the captain to save his passengers, except a few who were crowded together on a raft. After a long time at sea, further deaths and even instances of cannibalism, the survivors were finally rescued. Géricault made several studies of dying people and corpses in hospitals before executing this sublime painting – one of the greatest visual interpretations of human suffering.

THÉODORE GÉRICAULT
Rouen, 1781 – Paris, 1824
The madwoman, circa 1822
Canvas   77 × 64.5 cm
Presented by the Société des Amis du
    Louvre, 1938

THÉODORE GÉRICAULT
Rouen, 1781 – Paris, 1824
The plaster kiln, circa 1822/23
Canvas   50 × 61 cm
Purchased in 1849

THÉODORE GÉRICAULT
Rouen, 1781–Paris, 1824
The Epsom Derby, 1821
Canvas 92 × 122 cm
Purchased in 1866

Painted in 1821, during Géricault's stay in London, the
canvas takes its inspiration from English sporting prints,
which frequently depict horses at the 'flying gallop' shown
by the painter here. The invention of photography, by
allowing the various movements of a galloping animal to
be analysed, would allow it to be painted accurately, as
Degas was to do in his *Race-course* paintings.

113

A spectacular illustration of the enthusiasm aroused
amongst the romantic youth by the revolt of the Greeks
against the Turks, the *Massacre at Chios* was directly
inspired by the savage Turkish repression of the population
of the island of Chios in April 1822. The critics at the Salon
of 1824 received this fine painting very unfavourably.
Delacroix had been inspired by Constable's *Haywain*,
which was exhibited at the same Salon, reworking the
landscape background with a vibrant touch.

EUGÈNE DELACROIX
Charenton–Saint-Maurice, 1798 – Paris, 1863
The massacre at Chios, 1824
Canvas 419 × 354 cm
Purchased at the Salon of 1824

Eugène Delacroix
Charenton-Saint-Maurice, 1798 –
 Paris, 1863
The death of Sardanapalus, exhibited at
 the Salon of 1827/28
Canvas   392 × 496 cm
Purchased in 1921

Eugène Delacroix
Charenton-Saint-Maurice, 1798 –
Paris, 1863
Liberty guiding the people, 28th July 1830,
1830
Canvas   260 × 325 cm
Purchased at the Salon of 1831

EUGÈNE DELACROIX
Charenton-Saint-Maurice, 1798 –
    Paris, 1863
The sea from the cliffs at Dieppe, 1852(?)
Cardboard on wood   35 × 51 cm
Bequeathed by Marcel Beurdeley, 1979

EUGÈNE DELACROIX
Charenton-Saint-Maurice, 1798 – Paris, 1863
The women of Algiers, 1834
Canvas   180 × 229 cm
Purchased at the Salon of 1834

EUGÈNE DELACROIX
Charenton-Saint-Maurice, 1798 – Paris, 1863
Apollo vanquishing the Python, 1850/51
Mural painting   About 800 × 750 cm
Central panel of the vaulted ceiling of the Galerie d'Apollon
    in the Louvre

One of Delacroix's lesser-known masterpieces, the
subject-matter was dictated by its destination. *Apollo
vanquishing the Python* shows the painter working in a direct
line from the great decorators of the seventeenth and
eighteenth centuries, without losing any of his own ardour
or lyricism.

ARY SCHEFFER
Dordrecht, 1795 – Argenteuil, 1858
The ghosts of Paolo and Francesca appear to Dante and Virgil, 1855 (copy
  by the artist of a painting first executed in 1822)
Canvas   171 × 239 cm
Bequeathed by Madame Marjolin-Scheffer, 1900

HIPPOLYTE FLANDRIN
Lyons, 1809 – Paris, 1864
Young man by the sea, 1837
Canvas   98 × 124 cm
Entered the Musée de Luxembourg in
  1857

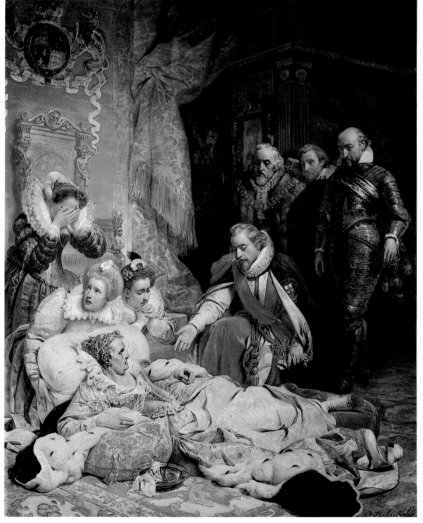

PAUL DELAROCHE
Paris, 1797 – Paris, 1856
*The death of Elizabeth I, Queen of
  England*, 1828
Canvas   422 × 343 cm
Purchased at the Salon of 1827/28

HORACE VERNET
Paris, 1789 – Paris, 1863
The gate at Clichy, 1820
Entered the Musée du Luxembourg in 1837

LÉOPOLD ROBERT
La Chaux-de-Fonds, 1794 – Venice, 1835
The Pilgrimage to the Madonna of the Arch, 1827
Canvas 142 × 212 cm
Purchased at the Salon of 1828

JEAN-BAPTISTE CAMILLE COROT
Paris, 1796 – Paris, 1875
Volterra, 1834
Canvas   70.5 × 94 cm
Bequeathed by Étienne Moreau-
    Nélaton, 1906

JEAN-BAPTISTE CAMILLE COROT
Paris, 1796 – Paris, 1875
Souvenir de Mortefontaine, exhibited at the Salon of 1864
Canvas   65 × 89 cm
Purchased at the Salon of 1864

JEAN-BAPTISTE CAMILLE COROT
Paris, 1796 – Paris, 1875
Chartres Cathedral, 1830, retouched in 1872
Canvas   64 × 51.5 cm
Bequeathed by Étienne Moreau-Nélaton, 1906

Jean-Baptiste Camille Corot
Paris, 1796 – Paris, 1875
Woman in blue, 1874
Canvas   80 × 50.5 cm
Purchased in 1912

The female figures executed by Corot entirely for his own enjoyment, particularly at the end of his life, are now often admired as much, if not more, than the landscapes for which he is traditionally famous. One of the last and perhaps the most beautiful of these female studies, unknown to the public during Corot's lifetime, is the *Woman in blue*, a triumph in the handling of paint and a fine example of strength of composition and grandiose simplicity.

Jean-Baptiste Camille Corot
Paris, 1796 – Paris, 1875
The interior of Sens cathedral, 1874
Canvas 61 × 40 cm
Gift of Jacques Zoubaloff, 1919

OCTAVE TASSAERT
Paris, 1800 – Paris, 1874
Studio interior, 1845
Canvas 46 × 38 cm
Presented by Ernest May, 1923

EUGÈNE ISABEY
Paris, 1803 – Montévrain, 1886
Beach at low tide, 1833
Canvas 124 × 168 cm
Purchased at the Salon of 1833

ALEXANDRE GABRIEL DECAMPS
Paris, 1803–Fontainebleau, 1860
The monkey painter, 1833
Canvas 32 × 40 cm
Thomy Thiéry bequest, 1902

ANTOINE-LOUIS BARYE
Paris, 1795–Paris, 1875
Lions near their den, c.1860
Canvas 38 × 49 cm
Thomy Thiéry bequest, 1902

THÉODORE ROUSSEAU
Paris, 1812 – Barbizon, 1867
Group of oak trees, Apremont, 1852
Canvas   63.5 × 99.5 cm
Bequeathed by Thomy Thiéry, 1902

CHARLES-FRANÇOIS DAUBIGNY
Paris, 1817 – Paris, 1878
The floodgate at Optevoz, 1859
Canvas   48.5 × 73 cm
Bequeathed by Thomy Thiéry, 1902

ALEXANDRE GABRIEL DECAMPS
Paris, 1803 – Fontainebleau, 1860
The defeat of the Cimbri, 1833
Canvas   130 × 195 cm
Bequeathed by Maurice Cottier, 1884

CONSTANT TROYON
Sèvres, 1810 – Paris, 1865
View from the heights of Suresnes, 1856
Canvas 182 × 265 cm
Thomy Thiéry bequest, 1902

One of Troyon's masterpieces and one of the most convincing statements of mid-nineteenth-century realism, the painting shows herds grazing on the slopes above the Seine, a broad loop of which is seen to the left. Troyon was then at the height of his fame and critics often compared him to the artists from the golden century of Dutch landscape painting.

Recent acquisitions 1980–1985

As a result of gifts, bequests and purchases, a number of important additions have been made to the collections of French paintings in recent years.

In the field of the Primitives, we should mention the acquisition in 1982 of the *Virgin of Sorrows* by Nicois Louis Brea, a rare artist of the transition from the fifteenth to the sixteenth centuries as yet unrepresented in the collections.

Seventeenth-century additions include a group of four still lifes by Linard, Moillon, Dupuis and Stoskopff, which were presented, with the *Winnowing of the Grain* from the School of Fontainebleau (p. 128), in 1982. Paintings by provincial artists hitherto unrepresented in the Louvre include the *Magdalen* by Guy François of Le Puy, and *Roman charity* by the Lorraine artist Charles Mellin, both acquired in 1985. The outstanding work to have come to the Louvre during this period is Philippe de Champaigne's striking *Arnauld d'Andilly*, offered to the Museum in lieu of death duty in 1979 (p. 130). The Schlageter and Kaufmann bequest of 1984 has brought the Louvre magnificent works by Vouet, Le Sueur and Bourdon, although the owners have retained a life interest.

It is the field of eighteenth-century paintings that the acquisitions have been especially significant. They include the *Portrait of Baretti*, a fine Subleyras given in 1981 by the Fondation Bella et André Meyer (p. 131), works by Nicolas Bertin, Roland Delaporte and two canvases by François-André Vincent. *Mercury and Argus* by Fragonard, after Fabritius, was acquired in 1981 (p. 131). Greuze's portrait of *Claude-Henri Watelet* (p. 133) was offered to the museum in 1982 and Chardin's *The canary* (p. 132) was acquired in 1985 and gives the Louvre an example of the inspired artist's late style of interior scenes. The splendid Schlageter and Kaufmann bequest includes some exceptional examples of Lemoyne, Boucher, Subleyras, Lagrenée, Greuze and Hubert Robert.

Nineteenth-century additions include canvases by Guérin and Granet (p. 134) and the bequest in 1981 of the portrait of the *King of Rome* by Prud'hon (p. 133). The collection of paintings from the period of the Restoration and the July Monarchy has received a number of important additions, including the *Sword of Henry IV* by Ingres, acquired in 1981 with the help of the Société des Amis du Louvre, Chassériau's *Andromeda* (p. 135), acquired in 1986, and the *Portrait of Madame Flandrin* offered by Madame Froidevaux, the great niece of the artist, in 1984 (p. 135). Other works include pieces by Alexandre-Evariste Fragonard, Papety and Delaroche. Finally, several sketches of ceilings for the 'Musée Charles X' by Blondel, Heim, Picot, Drolling, Meynier and Cogniet have been purchased.

SCHOOL OF FONTAINEBLEAU (circle of NICCOLÒ DELL'ABATE)
Winnowing of the grain, circa 1570?
Canvas 98 × 141 cm
Given in lieu of death duty, 1981

This poetic painting reflects the style of the landscape artist Niccolò dell'Abate, a painter who came from Bologna to Fontainebleau, where he worked with Primaticcio. It could be the work of Giulio Camilio, Niccolò's son, or it could be the work of a French artist working with him. The rustic subject is treated with an elegance and refinement that are typical of the Fontainebleau school.

LOUISE MOILLON
Paris, 1610–Paris, 1696
Cup of cherries and melon, 1633
Wood 48 × 65 cm
Given in lieu of death duty, 1981

SEBASTIAN STOSSKOPF
Strasburg, 1597–Idstein, 1657
Still life with books and a bronze statuette,
circa 1630
Canvas 51 × 69 cm
Given in lieu of death duty, 1981

PIERRE DUPUIS
Montfort l'Amaury, 1610–Paris, 1682
Plums and peaches on a table, 1650
Canvas 51 × 60 cm
Given in lieu of death duty, 1981

PHILIPPE DE CHAMPAIGNE
Brussels, 1602 – Paris, 1674
Portrait of Robert Arnauld d'Andilly, 1667
Canvas 78 × 64 cm
Given in lieu of death duty, 1979

The subject, a Councillor of State, withdrew to Port-Royal in 1646, from where he was driven out in 1660. His *Memoirs* appeared in 1667, the year in which the portrait, one of Champaigne's masterpieces, was painted. It has a unique simplicity and grandeur and displays a sharp understanding of the subject's character.

PIERRE SUBLEYRAS
Saint-Gilles, 1699 – Rome, 1749
Portrait, believed to be of Giuseppe Baretti, circa 1745
Canvas 74 × 61 cm
Presented by the Fondation Bella et André Meyer, 1981

JEAN-HONORÉ FRAGONARD
Grasse, 1732 – Paris, 1806
Mercury and Argus, circa 1765
Canvas 59 × 73 cm
Purchased in 1982

JEAN-SIMÉON CHARDIN
Paris, 1699 – Paris, 1779
The Canary, 1750–1751
Canvas 50 × 43 cm
Purchased in 1985

Commissioned for the king by Le Normant de
Tournehem, the Director of Buildings, and exhibited in
the Salon of 1751, *The Canary* subsequently became part
of the collection of the Marquis de Marigny, Madame de
Pompadour's brother. One of Chardin's last genre scenes,
it shows the painter influenced by Dutch art, using a
detailed language and a delicate balance of light.

Jean-Baptiste Greuze
Tournus, 1725 – Paris, 1805
Portrait of Claude-Henri Watelet, 1763
Canvas 115 × 88 cm
Given in lieu of death duty, 1981

Pierre-Paul Prud'hon
Cluny, 1758 – Paris, 1823
Portrait of the King of Rome, 1811
Canvas 46 × 56 cm
Given in lieu of death duty, 1982

MARIUS GRANET
Aix-en-Provence, 1775 – Aix-en-Provence, 1849
S. Trinità dei Monti and the Villa Medici, Rome, 1808
Canvas 48 × 61 cm
Anonymous gift, 1981

JEAN AUGUSTE DOMINIQUE INGRES
Montauban, 1780 – Paris, 1867
The sword of Henry IV, 1832
Canvas 32 × 28 cm
Purchased with the assistance of the Société
des Amis du Louvre, 1981

PAUL DELAROCHE
Paris, 1797 – Paris, 1856
Bonaparte crossing the Alps, 1848
Canvas 289 × 222 cm
Presented by M. and Mme. Birkhauser, 1982

HIPPOLYTE FLANDRIN
Lyons, 1809 – Paris, 1864
Portrait of Madame Flandrin, 1846
Canvas 83 × 66 cm
Presented by Madame Foidevaux, 1984

THÉODORE CHASSÉRIAU
Sainte-Barbe de Samana, 1819 – Paris, 1856
Andromeda and the Nereids, 1840
Canvas 92 × 74 cm
Purchased in 1986

Recent acquisitions 1986–1988

Once again, the acquisitions have been eclectic and designed to fill some of the gaps in the French collection.

In 1986 two important paintings enriched the French Primitives section: two undocumented panels by Nicolas Dipre— *The Birth of the Virgin* offered by the Amis du Louvre and the *Meeting at the Golden Gate*—now join *The Presentation of the Virgin in the Temple*, given by Pierre Landry in 1972 (see illustration p. 17) as part of the same ensemble.

The entry to the Louvre of the *St. Thomas* by Georges de la Tour after a public subscription which attracted great attention in the Spring of 1988, was one of those events which characterise the life of a museum. The last important work of the great Lorrain painter was still in private hands and a foreign buyer offered the French branch of the charitable works of the Order of Malta, a high price for it. The loss to the national heritage of this masterpiece seemed inevitable. The far-sighted attitude of the Order of Malta and the numerous generous gifts, whether modest or overwhelming, combined to secure the canvas for France, to hang close to *The Cheat*, the *St. Joseph in the carpenter's shop* and *St. Sebastian*.

Beside this now-popular masterpiece of French painting, the other acquisitions appear of secondary importance. These include *The Dawn*, an element of the decor of the chateau des Tuileries, painted by Jean Baptiste Champaigne, nephew of the more famous Philippe and above all the precious sketches of Eustache le Sueur for the five compositions of the *Cabinet de l'Amour* of the Hotel Lambert, of which the museum possesses the complete decorative scheme. Also worthy of mention is the sketch by Louis de Boulogne (the gift of D. Chereau, 1986) and the *Carrying of the Cross* by Largilliere (presented by the Amis du Louvre in 1988).

Two masterpieces by Fragonard dominate the eighteenth century acquisitions: *The Adoration of the Shepherds*, gift of M. and Mme. Roberto Polo, is the companion to the famous *The Bolt*, purchased in 1974 while the popular scene known as *The Beggar's Dream* was acquired as a gift in 1988, at the same time as a beautiful composition by Boucher, *The Marriage of Psyche and Cupid*. The *Portrait of Three Men* by Vincent is a rare example, painted in 1775, of artists in disguise.

For the nineteenth century, let us mention the gift by the Amis du Louvre of *The Funeral of Titian* (1832) by Alexandre Hesse, the purchase of the *Abbot of Bonard* painted in Rome in 1816, by Ingres.

NICOLAS DIPRE
Known at Avignon from 1495 – Avignon, 1532
The Birth of the Virgin, circa 1500
Wood 29 × 50 cm
Presented by the Amis du Louvre, 1986

This panel entered the Louvre at the same time as the *Meeting at the Golden Gate*, originally part of the same predella, to join the *Presentation of the Virgin in the Temple* given by Pierre Landry in 1972 (p. 17). The feel for geometric and angular forms and the direct lighting are typical of the Provencal school of painting.

GEORGES DE LA TOUR
Vic–sur–Seille, 1593 – Lunéville, 1625
St. Thomas circa 1625 – 30
Canvas 69 × 61 cm
Purchased with the assistance of public contribution, 1988

The acquisition for the museum collections of the *St. Thomas*, one of La Tour's 'daylight' masterpieces, was the outcome of a vigorous campaign and a public fund to prevent the canvas from leaving France. The bold, simplified modelling is combined here with a psychological analysis of rare subtlety. The refined sable and slate-grey colouring distinguishes the work from the five other La Tours in the Louvre, where reds predominate.

JEAN BAPTISTE DE CHAMPAIGNE
Brussels, 1631 – Paris, 1681
Dawn 1668
Canvas 144 × 189 cm
Purchased in 1986

EUSTACHE LE SUEUR
Paris, 1617 – Paris, 1655
The Birth of Love, sketch *circa* 1645
Canvas 26 × 63 cm
Purchased in 1988

Jean-Honoré Fragonard
Grasse, 1732 – Paris, 1806
The Adoration of the Shepherds, circa 1775
Canvas 73 × 93 cm
Gift of M. and Mme. Roberto Polo, 1988

Always considered one of the supreme canvasses of
Fragonard—it was the most expensive of the paintings sold
during his lifetime—and probably his most beautiful
religious painting, *The Adoration of the Shepherds* was painted
around 1775 for one of the great Parisian collectors, the
Marquis de Veri. Shortly afterwards he commissioned, as a
pendant—"in bizarre contrast", according to a critic of the
early xix century—the famous *The Bolt*, in the Louvre since
1974.

JEAN HONORÉ FRAGONARD
Grasse, 1732 – Paris 1806
Popular scene, known as *The Beggar's Dream, circa* 1768
Canvas 70 × 92 cm
Acquired as a gift in 1988

A major work by Fragonard, this picture, painted around 1768, is admirable for the bold handling and the warm, translucently glowing hues. But this very impetuosity poses the problem of its real subject: is it an old man dreaming of youth and domestic bliss represented by the group on the right? Or is it simply a nocturnal scene of the Italian *campagna*?

ALEXANDRE HESSE
Paris, 1806 – Paris, 1879
The Funeral of Titian 1832
Canvas 163 × 233 cm
Presented by the Société des Amis du Louvre, 1985

FRANCOIS-ANDRÉ VINCENT
Paris, 1746 – Paris 1816
Portrait of three men: the artist, the architect Rousseau and the
painter Van Wyck (?) 1775
Canvas 81 × 98 cm
Purchased in 1985

143

Index